美国人**365**天都在用的会话

啃书虫 编著

中国纺织出版社有限公司

图书在版编目（CIP）数据

美国人365天都在用的会话／啃书虫编著. --北京：
中国纺织出版社有限公司，2023.1

　ISBN 978-7-5180-9097-6

　Ⅰ.①美… Ⅱ.①啃… Ⅲ.①英语—口语—美国
Ⅳ.①H319.9

中国版本图书馆CIP数据核字（2021）第219840号

策划编辑：房丽娜　　责任校对：王蕙莹
责任设计：晏子茹　　责任印制：储志伟

中国纺织出版社有限公司出版发行
地址：北京市朝阳区百子湾东里 A407 号楼　邮政编码：100124
销售电话：010—67004422　传真：010—87155801
http://www.c-textilep.com
中国纺织出版社天猫旗舰店
官方微博 http://weibo.com/2119887771
三河市延风印装有限公司印刷　各地新华书店经销
2023年1月第1版第1次印刷
开本：710×1000　1/16　印张：14.75
字数：270千字　定价：39.80元

凡购本书，如有缺页、倒页、脱页，由本社图书营销中心调换

PREFACE
前言

　　现如今，人们无论是出国旅游还是职场工作，说一口流利的英语，能和外国人无障碍的沟通，已经成为现代人都想要拥有的一项技能。但是，很多中国人尽管已经学习了多年的英语，在需要张嘴说的时候，依旧是语无伦次、磕磕绊绊，一肚子想说的话，到了嘴边却表达不出来。

　　那么，怎么才能说好英语呢？编者认为，第一，要提高自身英语口语的储备量，多掌握一些口语的用法。第二，要敢于张嘴说，多说、多练、多模仿、多交流。当然，还少不了一本内容丰富、全面，发音地道、纯正的英语口语辅助教材。《美国人365天都在用的会话》这本书能够帮助你敲开英语口语学习的大门，并在口语学习的整个旅程中一路伴随你。

　　本书内容包括日常社交英语、职场商务英语和娱乐休闲英语三大部分，28个小节。收录的都是生活中常见的口语话题，还添加了很多热点和娱乐话题，增添了学习的趣味性，让你在学习的过程中不再枯燥无味。

　　《美国人365天都在用的会话》中的每个话题都设置了高频单句大放送、口语问答面对面、情景单词快记忆三个模块。从单词、短句开始入手，循序渐进地进入到情景对话中，让你更高效、全方位的掌握好英语会话。

　　本书具体特色如下：

　　内容全面、实用：本书所涉及的内容包罗万象，每个话题都是美国人365天都在用的。

　　简单易学：本书内容全部以中英双语呈现，每个单词、句子和对话均有中文翻译，降低了学习者的学习难度。

　　科学的学习方法：通过对句子、对话和词汇系统的学习，帮助学习者积累知识、融会贯通，扩大英语口语的储备量。

　　原汁原味的录音：本书配备纯正、地道的美式音频，学习者能够全方位地感受英语口语氛围并且进行跟读模仿，还有助于提升英语听力水平。

最后，编者衷心希望《美国人 365 天都在用的会话》这本书能够帮助大家学好英语口语，无论你遇到任何需要说英语的场合，都可以从容、流利地和别人进行交流。

编者

2022 年 10 月

CONTENTS
目录

第一章

日常社交英语

01 电话响起 Telephone

① 打错电话 Dialing a Wrong Number

● 高频单句大放送

01. Sorry, I think you have the wrong number.
不好意思，你拨错电话了。

02. Nobody here by that name.
这里没有那个人。

03. I must have dialed the wrong number.
我一定打错了。

04. I just moved here, so maybe the person you want lived here before me.
我刚刚搬来，所以或许你要找的是在我之前住在这里的人。

05. He probably changed to a new number. I'm sorry I bothered you.
他可能是换号了。很抱歉打扰你。

06. You have dialed the wrong number. Please look up the correct number in the telephone directory.
你打错电话了，请到电话簿里找正确的号码。

07. I'm sorry that I have disturbed you.
对不起，打扰了。

08. He doesn't live here any more.
他已经不住这里了。

09. Are you sure you dialed the right number?
你确定你拨的电话是正确的吗？

10. What number did you call?
你拨的是哪个号码？

● 口语问答面对面

A: Hello, can I speak to Ms. Li, please?
B: Ms. Li? There's no Ms. Li here. I think you have the wrong number.
A: 喂，请找一下李女士。

B: 李女士？这里没有姓李的女士。我想你打错电话了。

A: Is Patti there?

B: I'm sorry, I'm afraid you've dialed the wrong number. There is no Patti here.

A: 派蒂在吗？

B: 对不起，我恐怕你打错电话了。这里没有派蒂这个人。

A: Wrong number? Are you sure? I called yesterday and she was there.

B: I'm sure you have the wrong number. This one has been my number for more than 20 years.

A: 打错了？你确定吗？我昨天打这个号她还在呢。

B: 我肯定你打错电话了。这个号码我都用了二十多年了。

A: That's impossible. I remember the number clearly.Isn't this 7653456?

B: No, it isn't. It's 756-3456. It seems you've misdia-led.

A: 不可能的。这个号码我记得很清楚。不是765-3456吗？

B: 不是。是756-3456。看起来是你拨错了。

A: I'm so sorry I bothered you. I'll try again.

B: That's all right. This sort of thing happens all the time to everyone.

A: 对不起，打扰了。我再试一下。

B: 没关系。这种事情每个人都会碰到。

A: Sorry again for bothering you.

B: No worries.

A: 打扰了，再次表示歉意。

B: 没事的。

A: What number did you call?

B: 765-2365.

A: 你打的是哪个号码？

B: 765-2365。

A: Is Jack in?

B: Sorry, there is no Jack here.

A: 杰克在家吗？

B: 对不起，这里没有叫杰克的人。

A: He doesn't live here any more.

B: I'm sorry I bothered you.
A: 他已经不住在这儿了。
B: 很抱歉打扰你。

A: I'm afraid you've dialed the wrong number.
B: I'm sorry I bothered you.
A: 恐怕你打错电话了。
B: 很抱歉打扰你。

情景单词快记忆

beg 乞求；请求；恳求	pardon 原谅；请再说一遍
come on 来吧；快点；出现；上演	check 制止；控制；检查；核对
offer 提供；提出；提议；呈现；出现	type 打字
madam 夫人；女士；太太；小姐	store 贮藏；贮存；商店
goods 商品；货物；财产	suggest 建议；提出
phone book 电话簿	problem 难题；问题

② 电话留言 Leaving a Message

高频单句大放送

01. Do you want to leave a message?
    您想留言吗?

02. Do you want me to tell her you called?
    要我告诉她您打过电话吗?

03. Should I tell her you called?
    需要我告诉她您打过电话吗?

04. Do you want me to relay a message from you?
    您需要我帮您传达什么信息吗?

05. Does he have your phone number? How about giving it to me just to be sure?
    他有您的电话号码? 为了确保不出问题，要不您把电话号码告诉我?

06. Do you want him to call you back?
    您需要他给您打回去吗?

07. I'll put a note on his desk.
    我会在他的桌子上放一张纸条。

08. I'll give him the message as soon as he returns.
他一回来我就把留言告诉他。

09. Should I tell him what this is about?
需要我告诉他是什么事吗?

10. Would you tell him to call me at my office?
您能让他打我公司电话吗?

🔵 口语问答面对面

A: May I take a message?
B: Yes, can you tell him Mr. Park called?
A: 需要我替你传话吗?
B: 好的,你能告诉他帕克先生打过电话吗?

A: Any message for me?
B: Yes, Mr. Holt called and wanted to postpone your lunch meeting.
A: 有没有我的留言?
B: 有,霍尔特先生打过电话,他希望推迟和你的午餐约会。

A: I'd like to speak to Dr. Johnson.
B: Sorry, but he's not in. May I take a message for him?
A: 请约翰大夫接电话。
B: 对不起,他不在。我可以给他捎个口信吗?

A: This is Bob. Would you ask him to call me back, please?
B: OK, I'll tell him.
A: 我是鲍勃。请他给我回电话好吗?
B: 好的,我会告诉他的。

A: Hello. Is Bob there, please?
B: Hold on a second please. I'm sorry. He has gone out.
A: 你好,鲍勃在吗?
B: 请稍等。抱歉,他出去了。

A: When will he be back?
B: He will be back at about seven o'clock.
A: 他什么时候回来?
B: 大约七点回来。

A: Can I leave a message?
B: Yes, certainly.
A: 我可以留个口信吗?
B: 好的,当然可以。

A: Please tell him I'll call him at the office tomorrow afternoon.
B: All right. I'll tell him when he comes back.
A: 请告诉他明天下午我会往他办公室打电话。
B: 好的,他回来时我会告诉他。

A: Mr. Smith is expecting you at 3 o'clock.
B: Fine, I'll be there at three. Thank you.
A: 史密斯先生下午三点等你。
B: 好的,我三点到,谢谢。

A: Could I speak to your manager?
B: Sorry, but he is not in.
A: 我可以同你们的经理谈话吗?
B: 抱歉,他不在。

情景单词快记忆

operator 接线员,话务员	night call 夜间电话
switch board 交换台	service call 服务电话
extension (电话的)分机	area code 区号
telephone 电话	information 信息
telephone number 电话号码	ring tone 手机铃声
telephone book 电话簿	busy tone 忙音
telephone directory 电话号码簿	hold on (打电话时不挂断;口语)等一等;停住
international call 国际电话	picture phone 电视电话
overseas call 海外电话	call me back 给我回电
long distance call 长途电话	recording telephone 录音电话
emergency call 紧急电话	interception 窃听,侦听
public telephone 公共电话	push button 电钮,按钮;开关
station to station call 局间呼叫;叫号电话	message 信息,短信

person to person call 传呼电话；定人呼叫　　confirm 确认

collect call 被叫用户付费的电话　　　　　　local call 当地电话

caller 打电话者　　　　　　　　　　　　　　hang up 挂断电话

③ 挂断电话 Hanging Up

高频单句大放送

01. Something urgent has come up.
　　我现在有点急事。

02. Is that all?
　　说完了吗？

03. Thank you for calling.
　　谢谢你打电话过来。

04. I'll be off the phone in a minute.
　　我马上就得挂电话了。

05. My call to America has been cut off.
　　我打往美国的电话被切断了。

06. I won't keep you any longer.
　　我不再占用你的时间了。

07. Sorry, I'd better go now.
　　抱歉，我要挂电话了。

08. My other line is ringing.
　　我的另一部电话响了。

09. Give me your number, and I'll call you back.
　　给我你的号码，我过会儿给你打过去。

10. I'm too tired now. I have to go to sleep. Goodbye.
　　现在我太累了，我得去睡觉了。再见。

口语问答面对面

A: Something urgent has come up. I'd better go now.
B: OK.
A: 我现在有点儿急事。我要挂电话了。
B: 好的。

A: I will call you later.

B: Fine. Bye-bye.

A: 我待会打给你。

B: 好的。再见。

A: Thank you for your time. I'll hang up now.

B: You're welcome. Call me at any time.

A: 谢谢您抽出时间。我要挂电话了。

B: 不客气。你随时可以给我来电话。

A: Another line is ringing. I have to go.

B: OK. It's nice talking to you.

A: 另一部电话响了。我得挂了。

B: 好的，很高兴跟你通话。

A: Thank you. Bye.

B: Bye!

A: 谢谢你。再见!

B: 再见!

A: I'm too tired now. I have to go to sleep. Goodbye.

B: But…

A: 现在我太累了，我得去睡觉了。再见。

B: 但是……

A: There's someone on the other line. I have to go.

B: OK. It's nice talking to you.

A: 另一部电话响了。我得挂了。

B: 好的，很高兴跟你通话。

A: Thank you for your precious time. I'll hang up now.

B: You're welcome. Call me at any time.

A: 感谢您抽出宝贵的时间。我要挂电话了。

B: 不客气。你随时可以给我来电话。

A: Can I call you back? There is an emergency.

B: OK.

A: 我回头打给你好吗? 我现在有点急事。

B: 好的。

A: I'll get back to you later.
B: OK. Goodbye.
A: 我稍后给你回电话。
B: 好的。再见。

🌐 情景单词快记忆

local call 市内电话	three party service 三方通话
public phone 公用电话	conference service 会议电话
abbreviated dialing 快速呼叫	long distance call 长途电话
hot line service 热线服务	paging 寻呼
outgoing call barring 呼出加锁	mobile phone 移动电话
do not disturb service 免打扰服务	telegraph 电报
malicious call tracing 追查恶意呼叫	fax 传真
alarm-call service 闹钟服务	e-mail 电子信箱
call back 回叫	internet 互联网
call transfer 呼叫转移	local telephone office 本地电话局
call waiting 呼叫等待	telephone card 电话卡

读书笔记

02 美食天下 Food

① 在外就餐 Dining Out

🔵 高频单句大放送

01. I can't eat another bite.
我一口也吃不下去了。

02. I'm afraid I have no more room for dessert.
恐怕我已经吃不下甜点了。

03. It's too salty.
太咸了。

04. I never eat at fast-food restaurant.
我从来不在快餐店吃饭。

05. It's too greasy.
太油腻了。

06. It's not my taste.
不符合我的口味。

07. You want a little sugar with your iced tea?
你的冰茶里面还想再加点糖吗？

08. Give me the coldest beer you have.
给我你们这儿最凉的啤酒。

09. Make it weak.
要淡一点。

10. I don't go for ladies drinks.
我不喜欢女士饮料。

🔵 口语问答面对面

Marvin: This is a very nice restaurant.
Lucy: Really? Could you give me some advice on their dishes?
马文: 这是一家非常不错的餐馆！
露茜: 真的吗？可以给我推荐一下他们的菜品吗？

Marvin: I'd like to advise you to have some beef. They have a long history to
　　　serve it here.

Lucy: It means beef is a traditional dish here?

马文: 我想向你推荐牛肉。这家饭店供应牛肉已有很长的历史了。

露茜: 你的意思是牛肉在这里是很传统的一道菜?

Lucy: So I must taste it?

Marvin: Yes, exactly. They cook beef in a special way. I'm sure you'll certainly
　　　be quite satisfied with it.

露茜: 所以说我必须品尝一下?

马文: 是的，非常正确。他们的牛肉烹制方法与众不同，我保证你吃过之后一定很
　　　满意。

Lucy: That'll make it very delicious.

Marvin: Of course.

露茜: 这会使牛肉很可口呀。

马文: 当然。

Lucy: I am starving. I can't wait to pig out at dinner.

Marvin: Me, too.

露茜: 我饿了，真恨不得马上就有晚饭可以吃。

马文: 我也是。

Marvin: Let's order dishes as quickly as we can.

Lucy: Alright.

马文: 我们快点点菜吧。

露茜: 好啊。

Marvin: What would you like to have?

Lucy: I have no idea. Do you have any suggestions?

马文: 你想吃什么?

露茜: 我也不知道。你有什么好的建议吗?

Marvin: How about trying their specials?

Lucy: All right. Let's order.

马文: 尝尝他们的特色菜怎么样?

露茜: 好的，那我们点菜吧。

Marvin: Would you like a drink?

Lucy: I'd like to have a cup of coffee.
马文: 你想喝点什么吗?
露茜: 我想喝杯咖啡。

Marvin: How is it?
Lucy: Yes. This tastes great.
马文: 怎么样?
露茜: 确实很不错。味道很好。

🔵 情景单词快记忆

alcohol 酒精	appetite 胃口,食欲
artificial 人造的;仿真的	bland 淡而无味的;温和的;无刺激性的
chef 主厨;大厨	delicacy 佳肴
fragrant 有香味的;芳香的	ingredient 成分;配料;配方
liquor 烈酒(如威士忌)	munch 用力嚼;大声咀嚼
palatable 美味的;顺耳的;怡人的	portion 部分;一份
ravenous 饥饿的;贪婪的	refreshment 茶点
aperitif 饭前酒	appetizer 开胃菜
beverage 饮料	buffet 自助餐
chopsticks 筷子	dessert 餐后甜点
entree 主菜	hors d'oeuvre 开胃小菜
leftover 剩饭剩菜	menu 菜单
napkin 餐巾	pastry 用面团和油酥烤成的小甜点心
preservative 防腐剂	recipe 食谱;烹饪法;秘诀
seasoning 调味品;佐料	snack 小吃;点心
spice 香料;调味品	

② 在自助餐馆 Buffet

🔵 高频单句大放送

01. **What kind of main meals do you have on your buffet?**
自助餐的主食都有什么?

02. You can choose whatever you like.
你可以选择任何你喜欢的食物。

03. We have to wait in line in a cafeteria.
在自助餐馆我们要排队等候。

04. Food in a cafeteria is usually cheaper than in a restaurant.
自助餐馆里的饭菜一般比普通饭馆的要便宜。

05. This cafeteria always offers a big variety.
这家自助餐馆菜色总是很多。

06. It pays to go to the buffet when you are hungry.
饿的时候去吃自助餐是非常划算的。

07. Our main buffet table is over there. You can get silverware and dishes from there.
我们的自助餐桌在那边。您可以在那里取餐具和餐盘。

08. You can choose whichever you want.
你想要什么就选什么。

09. The buffet is over there. Please help yourself.
自助餐在那边。请自便。

10. This is a cafeteria. We have to serve ourselves.
这是自助餐馆。我们得自己动手。

🔵 口语问答面对面

Waiter: How is everything here?
Customer: Great. We're really enjoying the buffet.
服务员: 这里的菜怎么样?
顾客: 非常好。我们真的很喜欢这里的自助餐。

Waiter: Are you finished with these plates?
Customer: Yes, except for this one. I'm still working on it.
服务员: 这些盘子都用完了吗?
顾客: 是的，除了这个，其他的盘子都用完了。这个盘子里的，我还在吃。

Waiter: Would you mind if I took the rest of these plates away?
Customer: Not at all.
服务员: 您介意我把其他的盘子都撤走吗?
顾客: 不介意。

Waiter: Would you like me to bring you new ones for your next trip to the buffet?

Customer: Yes, please. That would be great.

服务员: 您希望我给您再拿几个新盘子吗，以便您下次去取食物?

顾客: 好的，那太好了。

Waiter: Can I get you anything else right now?

Customer: Actually, last time we went up, we noticed that the French fries were running low.

服务员: 您现在还要其他什么吗?

顾客: 事实上，上次我们去取食物的时候，看到炸薯条快没了。

Waiter: Thanks for letting me know. I'll go and get some more. I can bring a few slices to your table if you prefer.

Customer: That won't be necessary. Thanks.

服务员: 谢谢您告诉我，我去再加一些。如果您愿意的话，我给您再拿一些过来。

顾客: 不用了，谢谢。

A: What are you doing for dinner after work?

B: No plans. What did you have in mind?

A: 下班后吃什么?

B: 没什么计划。你想吃什么?

A: Let me take care of the check today.

B: Why? It's unfair. How about going Dutch?

A: 今天我来买单。

B: 为什么? 这样不公平。我们各付各的怎么样?

A: What's the damage?

B: It's 12 dollars and 80 cents altogether. But don't forget the tip. It's usually 15%.

A: 总共是多少钱呢?

B: 总共是 12 美元 80 美分。但别忘了还有小费，通常是总消费的 15%。

A: Hey, aren't you going to show us the bill?

B: Nope. Don't worry about it. I got it.

A: 嗨，你不打算给我们看一下账单吗?

B: 不用了，你们别管了，我已经付过了。

情景单词快记忆

tasty 美味的	delicious 味道好的
sweet 甜的	sour 酸的
bitter 苦的	hot 辣的
salty 咸的	spiced 加香料的
fragrant 香的	seasoned 加作料的
tasteless 无味的	greasy 油腻的
bland 清淡的	cafeteria 自助餐厅
snack-bar 快餐部，小吃店	ready-to-eat section 快餐部
dining-room 餐室	banquet hall 宴会厅
breakfast 早餐	lunch 午餐
luncheon 午餐，午餐会	supper 晚餐
snack 快餐	afternoon tea 下午茶点
refreshments 茶点	tea party 茶会
informal dinner 便宴	buffet（车站，火车内的）餐室，快餐柜，小吃店

③ 在快餐店 At the Fast-food Restaurant

高频单句大放送

01. What can I get for you today?
请问您要点什么？

02. Your French fries will be ready in a minute.
您的薯条马上就好。

03. I don't care for French fries.
我不喜欢炸薯条。

04. I'd like a hamburger with ketchup.
我要一个加番茄酱的汉堡。

05. I think I'll try their bacon cheese burger.
我想尝尝他们的咸肉奶酪汉堡包。

06. Would you like something to drink?
要点什么喝的吗？

07. Fast food restaurants are popular now.

现在快餐店很受欢迎。

08. Will you be eating here?
　　您是在这儿吃吗？

09. I'd like it to go, please.
　　不，带走。

10. Would you like a salad or a baked potato?
　　您要沙拉还是要烤土豆?

🔵 口语问答面对面

Waiter: Welcome! Can I help you?

Tom: I want a small order of French fries and a Big Mac.

服务生: 欢迎光临! 请问您需要点什么?

汤姆: 我要一小份炸薯条和一个巨无霸。

Waiter: Anything else? What about a strawberry pie?

Tom: No, thanks.

服务生: 您还需要其他的吗? 来一个草莓派怎么样?

汤姆: 不要了，谢谢你。

Waiter: Is that for here or to go?

Tom: For here.

服务生: 您是在这里吃还是要带走?

汤姆: 在这里吃。

Waiter: What would you like, sir?

Mike: I'd like an orange juice and two hot dogs.

服务生: 先生，您想要点儿什么?

迈克: 我要一杯橙汁和两个热狗。

Waiter: Is that all?

Mike: Yes, that's it.

服务生: 就这些吗?

迈克: 是的，就这些。

Waiter: Could you wait just a moment, please? Your hot dogs will be ready soon.

Mike: Sure!

服务生: 您能稍等片刻吗? 您要的热狗很快就好。

迈克: 当然可以。

Waiter: **Will you be eating here?**
Mike: **I'd like it to go, please.**
服务生: 您是在这儿吃吗?
迈克: 不，带走。

Waiter: **Is that for here or to go?**
Tom: **To go.**
服务生: 您是在这里吃还是要带走?
汤姆: 带走。

Waiter: **Anything else?**
Tom: **No, thanks.**
服务生: 还要其他什么吗?
汤姆: 不了，谢谢。

情景单词快记忆

big Mac 巨无霸	family big box 全家桶
ketchup 番茄酱	KFC plated meals 肯德基套餐
hamburger 汉堡	sandwich 三明治
cheese burger 芝士汉堡	mashed potato 土豆泥
grilled chicken filet burger 烧鸡柳汉堡	popcorn chicken 鸡米花
French fries 薯条	original recipe 原味鸡
apple pie 苹果派	corn salad 玉米沙拉
coca-cola(small) 小杯可乐	egg & vegetable soup 芙蓉汤
coca-cola(medium) 中杯可乐	dinner roll 餐包
coca-cola(large) 大杯可乐	chicken loaf 鸡肉卷
pineapple pie 菠萝派	fresh grade breast 鸡胸肉
baked apple pie 烤苹果派	Mc Chicken 麦香鸡
concentrated orange juice 浓缩橙汁	black tea 红茶

03 饮食文化 Food Culture

① 在咖啡馆 At the Cafe

高频单句大放送

01. **What kind of coffee would you like?**
你喜欢哪种咖啡？

02. **Why don't you drink coffee?**
你为什么不喝咖啡？

03. **I don't like the caffeine in the coffee.**
我不喜欢咖啡里面含有的咖啡因。

04. **How would you like coffee?**
你喜欢什么咖啡？

05. **A cup of black coffee, please.**
请来一杯黑咖啡。

06. **What do you recommend?**
你给我推荐一种吧？

07. **Would you like some dessert?**
您想要点甜点吗？

08. **Well, I'll have a small piece of cake.**
嗯，好吧。我来一小块蛋糕。

09. **What else are you going to have?**
您还需要其他的吗？

10. **What about a green tea or perhaps a coffee latte?**
你看绿茶或拿铁咖啡，怎么样？

口语问答面对面

Waiter: Good afternoon.
Tom: I'm Tom Johnson. We made a reservation for tea this afternoon.
服务生: 下午好。
汤姆: 我是汤姆·约翰逊。我们预订了今天下午用茶点。

Waiter: This way, please. Here's your table. Is this all right?

Tom: Yes, it's nice, indeed. Thank you.

服务生: 请这边走。这就是你们的桌子。您感觉还可以吗?

汤姆: 好极了! 谢谢你。

Tom: What would you like, Mike?

Mike: I'll try a chicken salad sandwich and have a cup of coffee with cream.

汤姆: 你想吃点什么,迈克?

迈克: 我想尝尝鸡肉沙拉三明治,并要一杯奶咖啡。

Waiter: How about you, Mr. Johnson?

Tom: I will have black tea with lemon and sugar and a piece of apple pie.

服务生: 那么您呢,约翰逊先生?

汤姆: 我要柠檬红茶加糖和一块苹果派。

Waiter: Anything else?

Tom: What's your special today?

服务生: 还要什么吗?

汤姆: 你们今天有什么特色菜?

Waiter: We have strawberries with cream today. I suggest you try them.

Tom: Good, I will.

服务生: 我们今天供应鲜奶油草莓。我建议你们尝尝。

汤姆: 好的,我想尝一尝。

Tom: Can I have some fruit instead of the dessert?

Waiter: Of course, you can.

汤姆: 可不可以不要甜点改要水果?

服务生: 当然可以。

Waiter: Anything else?

Tom: No, thanks.

服务生: 还要什么吗?

汤姆: 不用了,谢谢。

Waiter: What would you like?

Tom: I want some coffee and cold drinks.

服务生: 你想要点什么?

汤姆: 我想要点咖啡和冷饮。

Waiter: Anything else?

Tom: Yes, I'd like some apple pies.

服务生: 还要什么吗?

汤姆: 是的，我还想要一些苹果派。

情景单词快记忆

Coconut Mocha 椰子摩卡咖啡	Italian Coffee 意大利咖啡
Mango Mocha 芒果摩卡咖啡	Espresso 意大利浓咖啡
Banana Mocha 香蕉摩卡咖啡	Cappuccino 卡布奇诺
Iced Fruit Coffee 冰水果咖啡	Café Latté（Coffee Latte）拿铁咖啡
French Vanilla Coffee 法国香草咖啡	Café Americano 美式咖啡
Iced Coffee Float 漂浮冰咖啡	Decaffeinated Coffee 低因咖啡
Iced Chocolate Coffee 巧克力冰咖啡	Special Coffee（Mandeling and Brazilian Coffee）曼巴咖啡
Chocolate Coffee 巧克力咖啡	Instant Coffee 速溶咖啡
Charcoal Coffee 炭烧咖啡	Fresh Ground Coffee 现磨咖啡
Tres Rios Coffee 特雷里奥咖啡	Iced Coffee 冰咖啡
Vienna Coffee 维也纳咖啡	Iced Espresso 浓缩冰咖啡
Iced Swiss Coffee 瑞士冰咖啡	Iced Mint Coffee 冰薄荷咖啡
Brazil Coffee 巴西咖啡	Iced Cappuccino 冰卡布奇诺
Royal Coffee 皇家咖啡	Iced Caramel Cappuccino 冰焦糖卡布奇诺
Cointreau Coffee 君度咖啡	Iced Hazelnut Cappuccino 冰榛子卡布奇诺
Irish Coffee 爱尔兰咖啡	Iced Fruit Cappuccino 果味冰卡布奇诺
Ginger Juice Coffee 生姜咖啡	Fruit Cappuccino 果味卡布奇诺
Dame Coffee 贵妇人咖啡	Iced Café Latté 冰拿铁咖啡
Coconut Coffee 椰香咖啡	Iced Caramel Latté 冰焦糖咖啡拿铁
Colombian Coffee 哥伦比亚咖啡	Iced Vanilla Latté 冰香草咖啡拿铁
Jamaican Coffee 牙买加咖啡	Iced Hazelnut Latté 冰榛子咖啡拿铁

② 在面包房At the Bakery

🔵 高频单句大放送

01. There are many kinds of bread.
面包有许多种。

02. What kind of bread would you like?
你想要什么样的面包？

03. You can try this one.
你可以尝尝这种。

04. Is there a baker near by?
请问附近有没有面包店？

05. We were in luck, for the bakery was still open.
我们总算走运，面包店还开着。

06. The bakery serves us with fresh bread daily.
面包店每天都给我们提供新鲜面包。

07. Some bakeries provide French bread and cakes for people.
一些面包店为人们提供法式面包和蛋糕。

08. That's a bakery specializing in French pastry.
那是一个专门制作和销售法式蛋糕的面包店。

09. I must go to the bakery and pick up some rolls and cakes.
我必须到面包店买些面包卷和蛋糕。

10. Oh, the bread isn't fresh enough.
哦，面包不够新鲜。

🔵 口语问答面对面

Waiter: Welcome! Can I help you?
Tom: I would like some bread.
服务生: 欢迎光临! 请问你需要点什么?
汤姆: 我要买些面包。

Waiter: We have many different kinds of bread. What kind do you want?
Tom: Oh, let me see. I'd like some white bread.
服务生: 我们有好多种面包。您想要哪种?
汤姆: 让我想想。我要一些白面包。

Waiter: Here you are. Anything else?

Tom: I want some brown bread. I think brown bread is delicious.

服务生: 给你。还需要其他的吗?

汤姆: 我要些黑面包。我认为黑面包味道很好。

Tom: Is there buttered toast?

Waiter: Sorry, we've just sold out buttered toast.

汤姆: 这有奶油吐司吗?

服务生: 对不起，我们刚刚卖完。

Tom: What about French toast?

Waiter: Yes, but there is only a little left.

汤姆: 那么，法式吐司呢?

服务生: 有，但是只有一点儿了。

Waiter: There is only a little left.

Tom: That's all right. I'll buy all of it.

服务生: 只有一点儿了。

汤姆: 好吧。我要把它全买了。

情景单词快记忆

Garlic Bread 蒜蓉面包	Multi-grain Bread 杂粮面包
Loaf 佐餐面包	American Corn Bread 美式玉米面包
Rye Bread 黑麦面包	Russian Pumpernickel 俄式粗麦黑面包
Toast Bread 吐司面包	German Rye Bread 德国黑麦面包
Wheat Bread 小麦面包	Challah 犹太教白面包
White Bread 白面包	Danish Rye Bread 丹麦黑麦面包
Croissant Bread 牛角面包	French Toast 法式吐司面包
Black Rye Bread 黑麦面包	Donut 多纳圈
Bagel 面包圈	Bun 小圆面包
Baguette 法式长棍面包	Wholemeal Bread 全麦面包
Pita 皮塔饼	unleavened bread 无酵面饼

③ 野餐 Having a Picnic

高频单句大放送

01. Let's go hiking on Sunday.
星期天我们去徒步旅行吧。

02. Would you like to go on a picnic with us this weekend?
你愿意周末和我们一起去野餐吗？

03. Where shall we go for a picnic?
我们到哪儿去野餐？

04. No one else knows about this spot.
没人知道这个地方。

05. I enjoy camping.
我喜欢露营。

06. I'm looking forward to the picnic.
我盼望着去野餐。

07. Is everything ready for the picnic?
野餐的东西都准备好了吗？

08. The boys have decided to go camping next week.
男孩子们已决定下个星期去露营。

09. Hey, what about the outing?
嘿，对郊游感觉怎么样？

10. Rain put a damper on our picnic plans.
大雨阻止了我们的野餐计划。

口语问答面对面

Peter: It's so nice to have a picnic in such a lovely day.
Joan: Yes. Let's start right now. First of all we have to clean the grill.
彼得：这样的好天气来野餐真是太好了。
乔安：是啊，我们现在就开始吧。首先得把烤架洗干净。

Joan: Could you please take care of the grill while I go to collect some wood for starting a fire?
Peter: OK. Leave it to me.
乔安：你能去洗一下烤架吗？我去捡一些生火的柴。
彼得：好的，交给我吧。

Joan: We have enough wood now. Let's start the fire and begin roasting the chicken.

Peter: Good. Here are the chicken, oil, salt, and chili.

乔安: 柴火已经够了。我们生火，开始烤鸡!

彼得: 太好了。这里是鸡，还有油、盐、辣椒。

Peter: I'm going to prepare the plates. Call me if you need my help.

Joan: Fine. I can handle it myself.

彼得: 我去准备餐盘。需要帮忙的话叫我。

乔安: 好，我自己能搞定。

Peter: Oh, it smells delicious! I guess it's done now? Don't overcook the chicken.

Joan: It is still bloody inside. I should cook it through…OK! Come to have a taste of this tender, juicy chicken.

彼得: 噢，好香啊! 我猜已经烤好了吧? 不要把鸡肉烤得太熟了。

乔安: 鸡肉里面还有血丝呢，我该把它烤透一点……好啦! 过来尝尝这个鲜嫩多汁的鸡肉吧。

Peter: My mouth is already watering. Oh, it's fantastic!

Joan: I'm glad you like it.

彼得: 我已经在流口水了。噢，太棒了!

乔安: 你能喜欢我太高兴了。

Joan: Have you brought any drinks?

Peter: Yes, there is beer and orange juice in the cooler.

乔安: 你带喝的了吗?

彼得: 是的，冷藏箱里有啤酒和橙汁。

Joan: Do you need some pickles?

Peter: No, thanks. This is good enough!

乔安: 你来点泡菜吗?

彼得: 不用了，谢谢。这个已经够好了。

🔵 情景单词快记忆

cutting board 切菜板	spoon 勺子
fork 叉子	chopsticks 筷子

plate 盘子	bowl 碗
glass/goblet/cup/saucer 玻璃杯 / 高脚杯 / 茶杯 / 茶碟	disposable dishware 一次性餐具
tent 帐篷	napkin 餐巾
barbecue 烧烤	barbecue grill 烧烤架
charcoal 烤炭	spatula 扁平铲
pitcher 水罐	pepper/salt shaker 胡椒 / 盐瓶
skewer 肉串儿扦子	liver 肝
tuna 金枪鱼	sausage 香肠
ham 火腿	bacon 培根
mayonnaise 蛋黄酱	thousand island dressing 千岛酱
oil vinegar 油醋汁	ketchup 番茄酱
mustard 芥末	wasabi 青芥末
sashimi 生鱼片	sushi 寿司
caviar 鱼子酱	honey 蜂蜜
butter 黄油	cheese 奶酪
canned food 罐头食品	sandwich 三明治
hamburger 汉堡包	cereal 麦片
pasta 通心粉	spaghetti 细意大利面
pizza 披萨	toast 吐司
bun 小圆面包	white bread 白面包
whole wheat bread 全麦面包	roll 小长圆面包
baguette 长棍面包	donut 甜面包圈

读书笔记

04 社区服务
Neighborhood

① 在邮局 At the Post Office

🔵 高频单句大放送

01. How long does it take by regular mail?
普通邮件要多长时间？

02. Where would you like to send it?
您想寄到哪里？

03. May I send this letter by registered post?
我可以挂号邮寄这封信吗？

04. It usually takes about 3 days by airmail.
航空邮寄通常要 3 天时间。

05. It's quicker to use airmail.
航空邮寄比较快。

06. I need this to go express mail.
我需要寄快件。

07. I want to mail this parcel to China.
我想把这个包裹寄往中国。

08. Can it go as printed matter?
我能不能把它作为印刷品邮寄？

09. I'd like to pick up my package. This is the notice.
我想取我的包裹。这是通知单。

10. Please endorse it first.
请您先签收。

🔵 口语问答面对面

Jackie: Can I help you?
Maria: I want to send this package to Liverpool.
杰基: 有什么需要我帮您的吗？
玛丽亚: 我想把这个包裹寄到利物浦。

Jackie: **What does it contain?**

Maria: **A vase.**

杰基: 里面装的是什么?

玛丽亚: 一个花瓶。

Jackie: **By airmail or ordinary mail?**

Maria: **By airmail, though it's more expensive.**

杰基: 航空还是平寄?

玛丽亚: 航空吧，虽然比平寄要贵一些。

Jackie: **Do you wish to insure it?**

Maria: **Since it can be broken easily, I would like to insure it. I'll have it insured for 100 dollars.**

杰基: 您要上保险吗?

玛丽亚: 因为它易碎，我愿意投保。请给它保 100 美元。

Jackie: **You should fill out the form for the package and clearly state its content and value.**

Maria: **OK. How much should I pay?**

杰基: 请您填写这份表格并清楚地注明包裹内装有何物及其价值。

玛丽亚: 好的，我要付多少钱?

Jackie: **Let me weigh it first. Oh, the postage is 60 dollars.**

Maria: **Here is the money. Thank you.**

杰基: 我首先得称一下包裹重量。哦，邮资是 60 美元。

玛丽亚: 给你钱，谢谢。

Jackie: **How long will it take to get there?**

Maria: **About two days.**

杰基: 要多长时间能到那儿?

玛丽亚: 大约两天。

情景单词快记忆

post office 邮局	sub-post office 邮政支局 (美作: branch post office)
window 窗口	post-office box 邮政信箱
poste restante 留局待取 (美作: General Delivery)	cash on delivery 货到付款

pigeonholes 信函分拣台格架	sorting table 分拣台
mail sorter 信件分类装置	sorting office 信件分拣室
letter box 信箱（美作：mailbox）	letter-scales 信件磅
mailbag 邮袋	postman 邮递员（美作：mailman）
air mail 航空邮寄	parcel 邮包
diplomatic pouch, diplomatic bag 外交邮袋	express delivery letter, special delivery letter 快递信件
registered letter 挂号信	covering letter 附信
to register 挂号	to post a letter 寄信
delivery 递送	to deal with the mail 发信
collection 收信	acknowledgement of receipt 回执
by return of post 立即回信	writing paper 信纸
envelope 信封	addressee 收信人
consignee（包裹）收件人	payee（汇单）收款人
sender 发信人	address 地址
postal district 邮区	local 本埠
letterhead 印在专用印笺上头的单位名称、地址等	heading 抬头
date 日期	date stamp（加盖的）日期邮戳
postscript 附言，又及 (P.S)	please forward 请转发
postcard 明信片	circular letter 通知
printed matter 印刷品	money order, postal order 汇票, 汇单
telegraphic money order 电汇汇单	stamp 邮票
postmark 邮戳	franking 邮资
postage paid 邮资已付	exemption from postal charges 邮资总付
extra postage 附加邮资	

② 在办事机构 In the Administrative Office

🔵 高频单句大放送

01. I need marriage form, please.
我需要结婚登记表。

02. This window is closed. Next counter, please.
这个窗口已经关闭。请到旁边柜台办理。

03. Do you have all your paperwork with you?
所有文件都带了吗？

04. I need to renew my visa.
我需要更新签证。

05. Are you employed, or are you self-employed?
你是给别人打工还是自己当老板？

06. Do you have your own business?
你有自己的企业吗？

07. When did you find the body?
你什么时候找到尸体的？

08. When did you notice it was missing?
你什么时候发现它不见了？

09. The boy ran out in front of my car.
那个男孩冲到我的车前面。

10. If you remember anything more, contact us at this number.
如果你再想起任何事情，通过这个号码联系我们。

口语问答面对面

A: Is this the line for getting documents?
B: No, you need to take a number and wait until it's called.
A: 这里是在排队领文件吗？
B: 不是。你得领一个号，等着叫号。

A: Do you think you will catch the thief?
B: I hate to say it, but probably not. It's very difficult to catch this type of thief.
A: 你们能抓到这个小偷吗？
B: 虽然我不想说，但是很可能抓不到。这种小偷很难抓到。

A: We had a call about a burglary at this address.
B: Yes, officer. I called. Somebody broke through a downstairs window and stole a bunch of stuff!
A: 我们接到电话说这个地址发生了入室抢劫。
B: 是的，警官。是我打的电话。有人从楼下的窗户进来，偷走了好多东西。

A: How long do you plan to stay in this country?

B: I have a contract for one-year at this company.Here's the paperwork.

A: 你计划在本国逗留多长时间?

B: 我跟这家公司签了一年的合同。这是相关文件。

A: I'm not sure which form I need.

B: Well, I'll need to ask you a few questions first.

A: 我不知道我需要哪个表格。

B: 首先，我需要问你几个问题。

A: Is this the fire department? There's a fire across the street!

B: Please calm down and tell me your location.

A: 这是消防局吗? 街对面发生火灾了!

B: 请冷静一下，告诉我你在哪儿。

A: 911 emergency. State the nature of your emergency, please.

B: I think there's someone in my house! Send the police right away!

A: 911 紧急中心。请描述您的紧急情况。

B: 我想我的房子里有人! 请快点派警察过来!

A: Where do I go to pick up my passport?

B: Go to Counter Eight.

A: 我该去哪领我的护照?

B: 去八号柜台。

A: Are you single or married?

B: I'm single.

A: 你是单身还是已婚?

B: 我单身。

A: When did you notice it was missing?

B: One hour ago.

A: 你什么时候发现它不见了?

B: 一小时以前。

③ 在银行 At the Bank

高频单句大放送

01. I'd like to open a current account.
我想开个活期储蓄账户。

02. I'd like to open a checking account.
我想开个支票账户。

03. What's the difference between a savings account and a checking account?
储蓄账户和支票账户有什么不同？

04. You may open a current account with the bank.
你可以开一个活期存款账户。

05. Here is your passbook.
这是您的存折。

06. What's the interest rate for the savings account?
储蓄存款的年利率是多少？

07. The code is not correct.
密码错了。

08. How much would you like to take out of your account?
您想从账户上取多少钱？

09. I'd like to close my account.
我想清户。

10. How much would you like to remit?
您想汇多少钱？

口语问答面对面

Peter: Excuse me, I want to withdraw some money from my account. Here is my certificate.

Clerk: I'm sorry. The code number doesn't coincide with the one you gave us when you opened your account.

彼得：劳驾，我想从我的账户里取些钱。这是我的存单。

职员：很抱歉，密码与您开户时的密码不一致。

Peter: I'm terribly sorry. I can't remember it exactly. Let me see. Is this number correct?

Clerk: It's correct now. Do you want to withdraw all money from your account?

彼得：太抱歉了，我记不清了，让我想一想。这个号码对吗？

职员: 对了。您想把账户上的钱全部取出来吗?

Clerk: Actually you needn't cancel your account. I suggest you leave a small amount in your account so that you can keep it for further use.

Peter: That's not necessary. I'm leaving here for a long time and returning to my home country.

职员: 其实您不必销户的。我建议您在账户上留一点钱,您可以保留该账户,以便将来使用。

彼得: 没有必要了。我就要离开这里回国了。

Clerk: How would you like your money?

Peter: Can I have it all in one-hundred bills?

职员: 好吧,您需要什么票面的?

彼得: 都要一百元的,行吗?

Clerk: Here is your money and the interest you've earned. Please check it.

Peter: OK. Thank you.

职员: 这是您的钱和利息,请点一下。

彼得: 好的,谢谢。

Clerk: What can I do for you?

Peter: I'd like to open a current account.

职员: 我能为您做点什么?

彼得: 我想开个活期储蓄账户。

Peter: What's the interest rate on a new account?

Clerk: Here is a list of all the types of accounts we offer and the corresponding interest rates.

彼得: 新账户的利率是多少?

职员: 这里是我们所提供的所有账户类型列表以及相应的利率。

Clerk: How much would you like to take out of your account?

Peter: Two thousand dollars.

职员: 您想从账户上取多少钱?

彼得: 两千美元。

Peter: Can I have it all in one-hundred bills?

Clerk: Of course. Just a minute.

彼得: 都要一百元的,行吗?

职员：当然可以，请稍等。

情景单词快记忆

depositor 存户	a deposit form 存款单
a banking machine 自动存取机	to deposit 存款
deposit receipt 存款收据	private deposits 私人存款
certificate of deposit 存单	deposit book/passbook 存折
credit card 信用卡	principal 本金
overdraft/overdraw 透支	to cash 兑现
to honor a cheque 兑付	to dishonor a cheque 拒付
cheque/check 支票	rubber cheque 空头支票
cheque stub 票根	banker 银行家
resident 行长	savings bank 储蓄银行
Chase Bank 大通银行	National City Bank of New York 花旗银行
HongKong and Shanghai Banking Corporation 汇丰银行	central bank/national bank 中央银行
bank of issue/bank of circulation 发行银行	commercial bank 商业银行；储蓄信贷银行
member bank credit bank 储蓄信贷银行	discount bank 贴现银行
exchange bank 汇兑银行	issuing bank/opening bank 开证银行
confirming bank 保兑银行	paying bank 付款银行

读书笔记

05 奔波在外
Out

① 在书店 In the Bookstore

🔵 高频单句大放送

01. Have you got any English-Chinese dictionaries?
你们有英汉词典吗？

02. Would you like to have this one?
你想买这本书吗？

03. I'd like to buy an German grammar.
我想买一本德语语法书。

04. Those books are sold out now.
这种书现在脱销了。

05. Books of this kind are out of stock now.
这类书已被卖光了。

06. We're selling books on sale.
我们现在减价销售图书。

07. I'll take this one.
我买这一本。

08. Why do you buy so many books?
你怎么买这么多书？

09. Are these books on sale?
这些书打折吗？

10. We're having sales promotion in our store. All the books are on sale.
我们书店正在促销。所有的书都在打折。

🔵 口语问答面对面

Robert: Are you going to the bookstore today?
Tonny: Didn't we just go there last weekend?
罗伯特: 你今天去书店吗？
托尼: 上周末我们不是刚去过吗？

Robert: Today there will be a book signing in the store.

Tonny: What's the big deal! It's not the first time that someone signed his books at the store.

罗伯特: 今天书店有签售活动。

托尼: 有什么大不了的! 书店又不是第一次签名售书。

Robert: Today it's Professor Smith Adam.

Tonny: Really? I like his books very much.

罗伯特: 今天是史密斯·亚当教授。

托尼: 真的? 我非常喜欢他的书。

Robert: I'm going to get a book with his signature.

Tonny: I'll go with you.

罗伯特: 我一定要拿到他亲笔签名的书。

托尼: 我和你一起去。

Robert: There is a lecture on how to improve English in the bookstore today.

Tonny: How do you know they are holding such kinds of activities?

罗伯特: 今天书店有关于如何提高英语的讲座。

托尼: 你怎么知道书店在举办这些活动啊?

Robert: This bookstore always holds activities in order to motivate readers' interests in reading books.

Tonny: That's why the bookstore is always crowded with people.

罗伯特: 这个书店经常举办一些活动来激发读者的阅读热情。

托尼: 这也是为什么这个书店总是人满为患的原因。

情景单词快记忆

Chinese 语文	math 数学
English 英语	chemistry 化学
physics 物理	biology 生物
history 历史	politics 政治
geography 地理	art 美术
musicology 音乐	algebra 代数
geometry 几何	quiz 小测验

final examination 期末考试	entrance examination 入学考试
glue 胶水	satchel 书包

② 在加油站 At the Gas Station

🔵 高频单句大放送

01. My car's running out of gas.
   我的车没有油了。

02. Fill up the tank, please.
   请加满油。

03. What kind of oil do you use, sir?
   先生，您用哪种机油啊？

04. I have to have the car refilled now.
   我现在必须给车加油。

05. I guess I'll have to cut down my gas consumption.
   我想我也得降低油耗了。

06. Just give me four gallons, please.
   请给我加 4 加仑。

07. I also need you to check the engine oil and the radiator.
   我还需要你检查一下机油和散热器。

08. Could you fill it up with regular?
   请您给汽车加足普通汽油好吗？

09. May I fill it up by myself?
   我可以自己加油吗？

10. Is the gasoline in the tank enough?
   油箱里的油够用吗？

🔵 口语问答面对面

Henry: We need to stop and get some gas. I'm almost on empty.
Maria: You worry too much. We have plenty of gas to get home.
亨利: 我们需要停下来加点油。油表已经快指到"没油"了。
玛丽亚: 你太多虑了。我们还有足够的油可以回到家。

Henry: I don't think so. See, the warning light is on, too.
Maria: Usually after the warning light, there is about five gallons of gas left.

亨利: 我不这么想。你看，警示灯也亮了。

玛丽亚: 通常警示灯亮了之后，车子还剩5加仑油。

Henry: Really? There's that much?

Maria: Sure.

亨利: 真的? 有那么多吗?

玛丽亚: 当然了。

Maria: If it makes you feel better, we can stop at the Exxon there on the corner.

Henry: Good idea.

玛丽亚: 如果加油会让你觉得踏实点儿，我们就在街角那个埃克森加油站停下来加油好了。

亨利: 好主意。

Maria: I am absolutely sure that we have enough gas to drive home.

Henry: On the contrary, I feel so worried that my car will run out of gas on the middle of the highway.

玛丽亚: 我完全相信我们有足够的油供我们开回家。

亨利: 相反，我特别担心汽车会在高速公路上中途没油。

Maria: Could you fill it up with regular?

Henry: Sure.

玛丽亚: 请您给汽车加足普通汽油好吗?

亨利: 好的。

Maria: May I fill it up by myself?

Henry: Of course, you can.

玛丽亚: 我可以自己加油吗?

亨利: 当然可以了。

情景单词快记忆

industry lubricant 工业润滑油

high quality cylinder lubricants 高品质气缸油

hydraulic oil 液压油

brake fluid 刹车油

compressor oil 压缩机油

automatic transmission fluid 自动变速箱油

metal working oils 油性加工油

oil treatment 太空磁铀油精

gear oil 齿轮油

synthetic diesel engine oil 柴油引擎用油

turbine oil 涡轮机油	synthetic motor oil 汽车引擎用油
rust preventive oil 防锈油	all seasons 4T synthetic motor oil 全天候四行程机油
textile knitting oils 纺织机油	motor cycle gear oil 摩托车专用齿轮油
heat transfer oils 导热油	multi-purpose tractor oil 农机用油
refrigerator oil 冷冻机油	high temperature lithium complex grease 复合高温锂基润滑油
quenching oil 淬火油	auto grease 车用多效润滑脂
dielectric oils 放电加工油	low smoke engine oil 超强喷合油
lens grinding coolant 镜片研磨液	

③ 在图书馆 In the Library

高频单句大放送

01. The books are due back on the eighth of October.
这些书 10 月 8 日到期。

02. You can renew the book if you can't finish reading.
如果你没有看完这些书，你可以续借。

03. Can you tell me how to find books in the stacks here?
你能告诉我怎样在架子上找到书吗？

04. How long can I keep it?
我能借多久？

05. It's due two months from tomorrow.
从明天起再过两个月。

06. How many books am I allowed to check out?
我一次可以借出多少本书？

07. What if I'm not finished with it by the due date?
到了归还日期我还没读完怎么办？

08. I'd like to renew the book for another week.
我想续借一星期。

09. Please don't forget to return them by the due time. Or you'll have to pay fines.
请别忘了按期还书。否则你得受罚。

10. You'll have to pay the fine before you check those books.
在你借书之前你要先付清罚款。

● 口语问答面对面

Lauren: Good morning, can I help you?

Mia: Good morning. I want to look for some books for my dad.

劳伦: 早上好，有什么能帮您的吗？

米娅: 早上好，我想给我父亲借几本书。

Lauren: What kind of books does he like?

Mia: He is very fond of detective stories.

劳伦: 他喜欢什么类型的书？

米娅: 他很喜欢侦探故事。

Lauren: Has he read any detective stories before?

Mia: Oh, yes!

劳伦: 他以前读过侦探故事吗？

米娅: 噢，是的。

Lauren: Do you know if he's read this one?

Mia: I'm not sure, but he probably won't remember if he has.

劳伦: 你知不知道他是否读过这一本呢？

米娅: 我不太确定，但是他可能不记得他是否读过了。

Mia: He is very forgetful.

Lauren: Ah! He has a bad memory.

米娅: 他很健忘。

劳伦: 啊! 他记忆力不够好。

Lauren: How old is he?

Mia: He is seventy-seven.

劳伦: 他多大年纪了？

米娅: 77 岁。

Lauren: I suggest you take this book. It's very interesting.

Mia: Thank you. That's a good idea. He likes interesting books. Can you suggest another one?

劳伦: 我建议你借这本书。这本书很有意思。

米娅: 谢谢。好主意。他喜欢有意思的书。你能给我再推荐一本吗？

Lauren: What can I do for you?

Mia: I want to look for some books for my son.
劳伦: 有什么能帮您的吗?
米娅: 我想给我儿子借几本书。

Mia: How long can I keep this book?
Lauren: Please return your book(s) in thirty days.
米娅: 我可以借多久?
劳伦: 请于 30 日内归还图书。

Mia: Sorry, the books that you want are in circulation.
Lauren: Not at all.
米娅: 对不起，您要的书已借出。
劳伦: 没关系。

Mia: What if I'm not finished with it by the due date?
Lauren: You can renew the book if you can't finish reading.
米娅: 到了归还日期我还没读完怎么办?
劳伦: 如果你没有看完这些书，你可以续借。

情景单词快记忆

the national library 国家图书馆	municipal library 市图书馆
public library 大众图书馆	school library 学校图书馆
college library 大学图书馆	children's library 儿童图书馆
book card 书卡	book pocket 书袋
date slip 期限表	guide card 指引卡
subject card 主题卡	title card 书名卡
card catalogue 卡片目录	label 书标
stack room 书库	renewal 续借
book case 书橱	current issue 现期杂志
newspaper rack 报架	reading room 阅览室

06 人情世故
Social Relationship

① 家人团聚 Family Reunion

🌐 高频单句大放送

01. When there is a family, there is a god.
有家的地方就是天堂。

02. East, west, home is best.
金窝银窝，不如自家的草窝。

03. We never know the love of the parents until we become parents ourselves.
养儿方知父母恩。

04. There is a skeleton in every house.
家家有本难念的经。

05. We can't live without our family.
我们不能没有家。

06. You can tell your family everything because they are like your best friends.
你可以向家人敞开心扉，因为他们就像你最好的朋友一样。

07. My daughter gets my nose.
我女儿的鼻子和我的长得一模一样。

08. My mother is very gentle.
我的母亲非常温柔。

09. How do you think of your parents?
你如何看待你的父母？

10. My younger brother is still at high school.
我弟弟还在上高中。

🌐 口语问答面对面

Dennis: Is this a photo of your family?
Anna: Yes, it is. It was taken two years ago.
丹尼斯：这是你家人的照片吗？
安娜：是的。是两年前照的。

Dennis: Is anyone waiting at home to see me?

Anna: Of course! Your mother can't wait to see you again.

丹尼斯: 有人在家里等着见我吗?

安娜: 当然! 你妈妈都等不及要见你了。

Dennis: You look so lovely.

Anna: Everyone is lovely with his family.

丹尼斯: 你看上去很可爱。

安娜: 每个人和家人在一起的时候都很可爱。

Dennis: What does your mother do?

Anna: She is a teacher in a middle school.

丹尼斯: 你母亲做什么工作?

安娜: 我母亲是一个中学教师。

Dennis: Is she busy?

Anna: Yes, she is always very busy. We hope she can spend more time staying with us.

丹尼斯: 她很忙吗?

安娜: 是的,她总是很忙。我们希望她能花更多的时间与我们在一起。

Dennis: This must be your sister. What a pretty girl!

Anna: She won the beauty contest in her college.

丹尼斯: 这肯定是你姐姐。多漂亮呀!

安娜: 她是她们大学的选美冠军。

Dennis: Who is that young man beside you?

Anna: He is my elder brother.

丹尼斯: 你旁边的小伙子是谁?

安娜: 是我哥哥。

Dennis: Do you see your parents often?

Anna: Yes, I do.

丹尼斯: 你经常见你的父母吗?

安娜: 是的。

Dennis: What is your father?

Anna: He is a doctor.

丹尼斯: 你父亲是做什么的?

安娜: 他是一个医生。

Dennis: **Do you love your family?**

Anna: **Of course, I love them very much.**

丹尼斯: 你爱你的家人吗?

安娜: 当然了，我很爱他们。

情景单词快记忆

single 单一的；单个的；个别的	life span 寿命
marriage life 婚姻生活	bachelor 单身汉
spinster 大龄单身女性	husband 丈夫
wife 妻子	happiness 幸福
mother-in-law 婆婆	uxorious 疼爱妻子的
twin 双胞胎之一	daughter 女儿
son 儿子	maternal 母亲的
paternal 父亲的	children 孩子们
parental 父母亲的	filial 子女的
single parent 单亲	spouse 配偶
family 家庭	

② 走亲访友 Visiting Relatives and Friends

高频单句大放送

01. I paid a visit to Sally last night because I heard she was ill.
    昨晚我去看望了莎莉，因为我听说她生病了。

02. Today is Mother's Day. I've decided to go home to see my gerontic mum.
    今天是母亲节，我打算回家去看望我年迈的母亲。

03. During the Spring Festival visiting friends and relatives is a traditional custom for our Chinese people.
    春节的时候走亲访友是我们中国人的传统习俗。

04. For the family, she's an uninvited visitor.
    对于这个家庭来说，她是一个不速之客。

05. Next year I'll fly to Canada to see my aunt.

明年我打算飞去加拿大去看望我的姑姑。

06. The door bell is ringing, there must be someone visiting us.
门铃响了，肯定有人来拜访我们。

07. Get out of here, you're not welcome.
快走开，这里不欢迎你。`

08. I prepare to buy some fruits to see the little boy who had a car accident last week.
那个小男孩上周遭遇车祸了，我打算买点水果去看望他。

09. Don't forget to give me a call when you want to come.
你想来的时候不要忘了给我打一个电话。

10. This house hasn't received anybody for many years.
这间屋子多年没有人光顾了。

🌐 口语问答面对面

Bessie: Welcome to our home.

Jasmine: We're happy to be here.

贝西: 欢迎来我家。

茉莉: 很高兴能来你家做客。

Bessie: Please, have a seat. Make yourself comfortable.

Jasmine: This is a nice place you have here.

贝西: 请坐。不用拘束。

茉莉: 这个地方真是不错呀。

Bessie: Are you hungry?

Jasmine: No, we just ate on our way over here. Thanks.

贝西: 你饿吗?

茉莉: 不饿，我们在来这儿的路上刚吃过。谢谢。

Bessie: Can I give you a tour of the house?

Jasmine: Sure! I'd love to see it.

贝西: 我带你看看我的房子吧。

茉莉: 好啊! 我很想看看。

Jasmine: We really enjoyed visiting. Thanks for having us.

Bessie: It's been a pleasure.

茉莉: 我们这次来访很开心。谢谢你邀请我们。

贝西：我很高兴。

Bessie: Do you have to leave so soon?
Jasmine: I would love to stay, but I really have to get back.
贝西：你真的这么急着走吗?
茉莉：我也想再待一会儿，但是我必须回去了。

Jasmine: I'm glad you could make it.
Bessie: We'll have to have you over one of these days.
茉莉：很高兴你们能来。
贝西：改天也请你去我们家。

情景单词快记忆

lineage 宗族；世系	stock 门第；血统
generation 代	branch 支；系
tribe 部族；部落	clan 氏族
race/breed 种族	of noble birth 贵族出身
of humble birth 平民出身	dynasty 朝代
origin 出身	ancestry 祖先；先辈
ancestor/forebear/forefather 祖先	extraction 家世
descent/offspring 后代；后辈	descendant 后代；晚辈
progeny/issue 后裔	succession 继承
relation/relative/kinfolk/kin 亲属	my family 我家
my people 我家人	next of kin 近亲
family life 家庭生活	caste 社会地位

③ 邻里关系 Neighborhood

高频单句大放送

01. I just met our new neighbors.
我刚刚遇到我们的新邻居了。

02. My neighbor is a man of highest virtue.
我的邻居是一个品德高尚的人。

03. She petitioned her neighbor to turn down the radio.
她请求邻居把收音机关小点声。

04. She entrusted the care of her children to a neighbor.
她委托邻居照顾她的孩子。

05. His neighbor is a doctor.
他的邻居是一个医生。

06. He lives somewhere in the neighborhood.
他住在附近某处。

07. There is no such man in our neighborhood.
在我们的邻近没有这样的人。

08. The whole neighborhood praises him.
街坊邻居都称赞他。

09. She loves to gossip about her neighbors.
她喜欢议论邻居们的是非长短。

10. He lives next to me.
他住在我家隔壁。

🌐 口语问答面对面

Frank: Excuse me, can these gloves be yours?
Alice: Oh, yes. Thank you.
弗兰克: 打扰了，这副手套是你的吗?
艾莉丝: 哦，是的，谢谢你。

Frank: I saw them in the phone booth immediately after you left.
Alice: I was in a great hurry, and I wasn't aware that I had left them behind.
弗兰克: 你一离开电话亭，我就发现了。
艾莉丝: 我很匆忙，没有意识到把它们落下了。

Frank: My name is Frank Sullivan. I live in this apartment building. Do you live here, too? You must be new here.
Alice: Yes. I moved in only yesterday. My name is Alice.
弗兰克: 我叫弗兰克·沙利文，住在这幢楼。你也住在这儿吗? 你一定是刚来这儿吧。
艾莉丝: 对，我昨天刚搬来。我叫艾莉丝。

Frank: So we're neighbors. Call me Frank. I live in No. 303, and you?
Alice: I live No. 403.
弗兰克: 这么说我们是邻居了。叫我弗兰克好了。我住在 303 号，你呢?

艾莉丝: 我住在 403 号。

Frank: How interesting! That's right over us.

Alice: I hope I've not been making too much noise. I've just arrived from California and have got to move the things about a bit.

弗兰克: 真巧! 正好在我们楼上。

艾莉丝: 但愿我没有弄出太大的声音。我刚从加利福尼亚来这儿,我得把屋里的东西搬动一下。

Frank: No. By the way, why not drop in for a drink this evening? My wife Kathy would be most pleased to meet you. You can shoot the breeze with her. She is an easy-going person.

Alice: Thank you. I'd love to. See you in the evening then, Frank.

弗兰克: 没事。顺便问一下,有没有兴趣今天晚上到我那儿喝点什么? 我妻子凯西会非常高兴见到你的。你可以和她聊聊天。她是个很好接触的人。

艾莉丝: 谢谢。好的。那么今晚见,弗兰克。

情景单词快记忆

easy-going 容易相处的	adaptable 适应性强的
kind-hearted 好心的	amiable 和蔼可亲的
lazy 懒散的	amicable 友好的
diligent 勤奋的	analytical 善于分析的
energetic 精神饱满的	apprehensive 有理解力的
generous 慷慨的	aspiring 有志气的;有抱负的
intelligent 有才智的	capable 有能力的;有才能的
optimistic 乐观	cooperative 有合作精神的
independent 独立的	faithful 守信的;忠诚的
out-going 外向的	

读书笔记

07 生活花絮
Daily Conversation

① 天气 Weather

🔵 高频单句大放送

01. The weather is abnormal this year.
今年的天气不正常。

02. It's raining hard.
雨下得很大。

03. Snow covered the ground.
积雪覆盖了大地。

04. Snow is falling all over the country.
全国各地都在下雪。

05. Have you listened to the weather forecast?
你听天气预报了吗?

06. What's the temperature today?
今天的气温多高?

07. The fog cleared off.
雾气已散。

08. It's cloudy today.
今天阴天。

09. It's a find day today.
今天的天气真好。

10. Cold weather, isn't it?
天气很冷，不是吗?

🔵 口语问答面对面

Cathy: It is boiling today, isn't it?
Kayla: Yes, it's very hot and stuffy.
凯茜: 今天的天气热得要命，是不是?
凯拉: 是的，今天天气很闷热。

Kayla: It's sunny today, isn't it?

Cathy: Yeah, it's breezy today.

凯拉: 今天天气真好，不是吗?

凯茜: 是啊，今天风和日丽的。

Kayla: There are thick black clouds in the sky now. The wind is rising.

Cathy: It looks as if a thunder storm is coming.

凯拉: 现在天空乌云密布。刮风了。

凯茜: 看起来一场雷雨即将来临。

Kayla: Have you listened to the weather forecast?

Cathy: Yes, it is sunny today.

凯拉: 你听天气预报了吗?

凯茜: 听了，今天天气晴朗。

Kayla: How's the weather today?

Cathy: It's chilly today.

凯拉: 今天天气怎样?

凯茜: 今天冷飕飕的。

Kayla: Is it going to rain today?

Cathy: I heard it might rain.

凯拉: 今天会下雨吗?

凯茜: 我听说今天可能下雨。

Kayla: I'm sensitive to heat.

Cathy: You should take a hat.

凯拉: 我怕热。

凯茜: 你应该戴顶帽子。

Cathy: It's beginning to sprinkle.

Kayla: The weatherman says some showers are expected this afternoon.

凯茜: 开始下小雨了。

凯拉: 天气预报说今天下午将有阵雨。

Cathy: It's turning warmer, isn't it?

Kayla: Yes, the temperature is going up today. The temperature has climbed to 36℃.

凯茜: 天气在转暖，是不是?

凯拉: 是的，今天气温在上升。已上升到 36 摄氏度了。

Cathy: After a heavy rain, the temperature should drop a lot.

Kayla: Yes, there will be a cool day tomorrow.

凯茜: 大雨过后，气温会降很多。

凯拉: 是的，明天会是个凉爽的日子。

Cathy: What's the forecast for tomorrow?

Kayla: It's going to be cold.

凯茜: 明天的天气怎样？

凯拉: 会冷。

🌐 情景单词快记忆

abnormal weather 反常天气	changeable 多变的
change 变化	chilly 阴冷的
clear sky 晴空万里	cool air 凉爽空气
cool 凉爽的	hot weather 酷暑
lovely 可爱的	mountain 山脉
nice 晴好的	prefer 更喜欢
rainy 下雨的	spring 春季
sunny 阳光充足的	sunshine 阳光
umbrella 雨伞	warm and fine 晴和温暖
wonder 想知道	beautiful 美丽的

② 择偶 Choosing a Mate

🌐 高频单句大放送

01. As a man, he should be responsible and loyal.
    作为男人，他应该有责任心并且要忠诚。

02. I like man who is clever, witty and aggressive.
    我喜欢聪明、机智、有进取心的男人。

03. I can't stand a man who smokes and drinks a lot.
    我忍受不了好烟嗜酒的男人。

04. What's the most important trait that you think men should have?
你认为男人应该具有的最重要的品质是什么?

05. I dislike the men who are keenly alive to their own interests.
我讨厌斤斤计较个人利益的男人。

06. No one wants to marry a vulgar shrew.
没人愿意和一个粗俗的泼妇结婚。

07. I'm not interested in women who always nag about trifles.
我对那些总为小事唠叨的女人没兴趣。

08. I hope I can have an ideal wife: soft, pretty, good family, educated.
我希望能有一个理想的妻子，她温柔、漂亮、家世好、有教养。

09. You need a guy with an open mind, open pockets and no extended family.
你需要的男人要心胸宽广、慷慨大方、没有大家庭累赘。

10. You are more suitable for a man from the same culture.
你更适合来自同一文化的男人。

🔵 口语问答面对面

A: What kind of guy do you like?
B: I guess I like man who are funny. Someone who can make me laugh and relax a bit. They should be clever, witty and aggressive.
A: 你喜欢什么类型的男人?
B: 我想我喜欢风趣的男人。那种能让我开怀大笑、感觉稍微有点放松的男人。并且聪明、机智，有进取心。

A: What's the most important trait that you think men should have?
B: Loyalty and responsibility. I don't care much for personal wealth.
A: 你认为男人应该具有的最重要的品质是什么?
B: 忠诚和责任感。我并不在乎他的个人财产。

A: What about his appearance?
B: He should be tall, muscular and handsome.
A: 那外貌长相呢?
B: 他应该高大、健壮而且帅气。

A: What kind of man are not to your liking?
B: I hate man who always think they are right and are keenly alive to their interests, like you.
A: 什么样的男人你不喜欢呢?

B: 我厌恶那些总是自以为是并且斤斤计较个人利益的男人，就像你这样的。

A: What's up? You look depressed.

B: I just broke up with Daniel. Now I'm thinking about what kind of guy I'll end up with.

A: 怎么了? 你看上去很沮丧。

B: 我刚刚和丹尼尔分手了。现在我在想我最终会和什么样的男人在一起。

A: What kind of woman do you like?

B: I like woman who is warm, sexy and passionate.

A: 你喜欢什么样的女人?

B: 我喜欢温婉、性感、热情的女人。

A: I hear they're seeing each other.

B: I'm not surprised. Like attracts like.

A: 听说他们在交往。

B: 我不觉得意外，所谓物以类聚，人以群分。

A: Are you going steady?

B: Yes, we are.

A: 你们关系很稳定吧?

B: 是啊。

A: How long have you been dating, with Jack?

B: We've been dating for months.

A: 你和杰克交往多久了?

B: 我们已经交往几个月了。

A: I hate guys who take liberties with women.

B: So do I. I like those guys who are bold but cautious.

A: 我讨厌男人对女人动手动脚。

B: 我也是。我喜欢那种胆大心细的人。

情景单词快记忆

frank 直率的；真诚的	genteel 有教养的
gentle 有礼貌的	humorous 有幽默的
sensible 明白事理的	sweet-tempered 性情温和的

liberal 心胸宽大的	attractive 迷人的
lovely 可爱的	pretty 漂亮的
charming 魅力四射的	sexy 性感的
hot 火辣的	comely 清秀的
cute 可爱伶俐的	delicate 纤弱的
dreamboat 梦中情人	elegant 优雅的
eyeful 养眼的	foxy 古灵精怪的
pulchritudinous 貌美如花的	tasteful 风雅的

3 吸烟 Smoking

高频单句大放送

01. The first wealth is health.
健康是人生的第一财富。

02. I'm going to stop smoking when I finish this pack of cigarettes.
等我抽完这包烟我就戒烟。

03. I've decided to give up smoking.
我已经决定戒烟了。

04. Smoking is bad for your health.
吸烟有害健康。

05. Smoking is a nasty habit.
吸烟是个坏习惯。

06. How do you know you can give up smoking?
你怎么知道你戒得掉烟呢？

07. This is a non-smoking section, isn't it?
这是一个禁烟区，是不是？

08. Do you feel like a smoke?
你想抽支烟吗？

09. Do you mind my smoking here?
你介意我在这儿抽支烟吗？

10. Are you smoking a lot?
你抽烟很多吗？

🔵 口语问答面对面

Emma: When did you start smoking and why?

Daniel: I started smoking when I was 17. At that time, some of my friends smoked and they thought smoking was the "grown-up" thing to do.

爱玛: 你什么时候开始吸烟的? 为什么?

丹尼尔: 我 17 岁的时候开始吸烟的。那时候我的一些朋友吸烟,并且他们认为吸烟是长大的表现。

Emma: So you joined them?

Daniel: Most of us didn't know that smoking was bad for our health and for the health of people who were around smokers.

爱玛: 因此你就加入了他们的队伍?

丹尼尔: 我们当中的大部分人都不知道吸烟有害自己的健康,也有害于我们身边的人的健康。

Emma: But why do you continue smoking after you know smoking is bad for our health?

Daniel: Smoking makes me feel relaxed and it also helps me to calm when I am under pressure.

爱玛: 但是在你知道吸烟有害健康以后为什么还要吸呢?

丹尼尔: 吸烟让我觉得很轻松,并且当我有压力的时候,它能帮助我平静下来。

Emma: We all know that the more you smoke, the more you feel the need to smoke.

Daniel: Yes, exactly.

爱玛: 我们都知道吸得越多,烟瘾越大。

丹尼尔: 是的,确实是这样。

Emma: Why don't you stop smoking?

Daniel: I have tried several times, but it is really difficult.

爱玛: 你为什么不戒烟呢?

丹尼尔: 我试过好几次了,但是真的很难。

Emma: Smoking is really bad for our health, and cigarettes cost a lot of money which could have been used for other healthier things. So you'd better try your best to stop smoking.

Daniel: I agree with you.

爱玛: 吸烟对健康真的很不好，吸烟会花很多钱，而这些钱本来可以用于其他更健康的东西上面的。所以你最好努力把戒烟掉。

丹尼尔: 我同意。

🔵 情景单词快记忆

smoke 吸烟	tobacoo 烟草
cigarettes 香烟	nicotine 尼古丁
smoker 吸烟者	cigar 雪茄
non-smoking 禁烟	addicted to nicotine 对尼古丁上瘾
give up smoking 戒烟	hazards of smoking 抽烟的危害
stop smoking 戒烟	risks of smoking 抽烟的风险
harmful 有害的	TAHRI (Tobacco and Health Research Institute) 烟草和健康研究院
prohibit 禁止	RTDA (Retail Tobacco Dealers of America) 美国烟草零售商
banning 法律	NURT (National Union of Retail Tobacconists) 全国烟草零售商联合会

读书笔记

08 美从身生 Body Beauty

① 整形手术 Plastic Surgery

🔵 高频单句大放送

01. Plastic surgery is very popular.
整形手术非常流行。

02. I heard most of the Korean actresses have had plastic surgery.
我听说大多数的韩国女演员都做过整形手术。

03. Many people suspect that she has had a breast enlargement surgery.
很多人都怀疑她做过丰胸手术。

04. I'm ready for a lift.
我准备好去做拉皮了。

05. Last month she had a double eyelid operation.
上个月她做了一个双眼皮手术。

06. I still remember she's moon-face, but now is the oval face .
我记得她是圆脸的，但现在是瓜子脸了。

07. It is becoming increasingly popular over time.
随着时间的推移，它变得越来越流行了。

08. Many people are concerned with their looks and their lack of beauty.
许多人关注他们的外貌和长相的不足。

09. It is certainly not a good thing to do for young people who are still developing their face features.
对于年轻人来说改善他们的面部特征当然是不益的。

10. Sometimes plastic operation is necessary if your job position requires it.
如果你的工作需要，有时整形手术也是必要的。

🔵 口语问答面对面

Grace: Hi, James. Haven't seen you for ages. How are you getting along recently?

James: Nothing special. And you?

格蕾丝: 嗨，詹姆斯。好久不见了。最近过得怎么样啊?
詹姆斯: 没什么特别的。你呢?

Grace: Did you hear something about Jane?
James: Actually I haven't seen her for a long time. Do you know what's she doing?
格蕾丝: 你有听说关于简的消息吗?
詹姆斯: 事实上我好久都没见到她了。你知道她现在在干什么吗?

Grace: I heard she has gone to Korea to do the plastic surgery.
James: Oh, my god! I just can't believe it. I just hear about the plastic surgery on the TV and never think it will happen around us.
格蕾丝: 我听说她到韩国去做整形手术了。
詹姆斯: 哦，我的天哪! 真是不敢相信。我只是从电视上听过整形手术，从没想过它会发生在自己周围。

James: Plastic surgery is very popular.
Grace: Because it can make people pretty.
詹姆斯: 现在整形手术非常流行。
格蕾丝: 因为它可以使人变漂亮。

Grace: It has been very popular in domestic in recent years. And the shaping technique is the most advanced in South Korea.
James: I heard that almost most of the Korean actresses have had the operation.
格蕾丝: 这在国内近几年非常流行。并且韩国的整形手术是最先进的。
詹姆斯: 我听说基本上大部分的韩国女星都做过整形术。

Grace: I still like the natural beauty. They look healthier. I think the actresses of South Korea are largely identical except slight differences.
James: I'm the same with you. But may Jane have a successful operation.
格蕾丝: 我仍然喜欢自然美女。她们看起来更加健康。我感觉韩国女明星们都大同小异。
詹姆斯: 我和你的想法是一样的。但是还是要祝愿简手术成功。

② 美容 Beauty

高频单句大放送

01. Let me show you how to use it.
让我给你示范一下怎么使用。

02. It's a world-famous brand.
这是国际名牌。

03. This lipstick is always out of stock, there is not much left.
这款口红非常热销，已所剩不多了。

04. It has been a very popular lipstick this season.
这个季节那种颜色的口红一直很受欢迎。

05. What are the benefits of this mask?
这种面膜有什么功效？

06. I'd like a visible whitening mask.
我要美白效果明显一点的面膜。

07. I'm going to the beauty parlor this afternoon.
我今天下午去美容院。

08. How often do you go to the beauty parlor?
你多长时间去一次美容院？

09. Most facials start with a thorough cleaning.
面部美容大都是先彻底清洁面部皮肤。

10. I have tons of cosmetics and I use them all the time.
我有一堆化妆品并且我一直都在用。

口语问答面对面

Clerk: Good morning, madam. Can I help you?
Customer: I want to buy some cleansing milk.
店员: 上午好，女士。我能为您效劳吗？
顾客: 我想买洗面奶。

Customer: What would you recommend?
Clerk: Your complexion is on the oily side. I suggest you use cleansing gel.
顾客: 你能给我推荐一款吗？
店员: 您的皮肤比较油，我建议您用洁面啫喱。

Customer: Anything that can keep my skin clean will do.

Clerk: How about this one? It cleans thoroughly without striping your natural
　　　protective oil. The gentle formula keeps skin soft and healthy.

顾客: 任何能保持我面部清洁的都行。

店员: 这个怎么样? 它能彻底清洁您的皮肤, 又不会洗去保护表皮的天然油分, 而且
　　　配方温和, 能保持皮肤柔软、健康。

Customer: Hm…the smell is too strong, and I can't stand it. I'm very sensitive
　　　　　to fragrance.

Clerk: We've also got a fragrance-free one, especially for sensitive skin. I'm
　　　sure you'll like it.

顾客: 嗯……这个味道太浓了, 我受不了。我对香味非常敏感。

店员: 我们有一款无香味的, 是专为敏感肌肤设计的, 相信您一定喜欢。

Customer: I'll try that. Do you have facial cream to go with that?

Clerk: Yes, sure. This line of products is fragrance-free. We have facial mask,
　　　moisturizing lotion, eye cream.

顾客: 那我试试看, 有与之配套的面霜吗?

店员: 当然有。这个系列的产品都是无香味的, 包括面膜、保湿乳液、眼霜。

Customer: I'll buy the moisturizing lotion and cleansing gel first. If they suit
　　　　　me, I'll come back for the others later.

Clerk: Thank you very much, madam. Here are some samples of our products.
　　　Do try them out.

顾客: 我先买保湿乳液和洁面啫喱。要是合适, 再回来买其他产品。

店员: 谢谢您, 女士。这儿有一些我们其他产品的样品, 试试看。

情景单词快记忆

facial cleanser 洗面奶	toner/astringent 爽肤水
firming lotion 紧肤水	toner/smoothing toner 柔肤水
cream 护肤霜	moisturizer 保湿
sun screen/sun block 隔离霜; 防晒霜	whitening 美白
lotion 露	body wash 沐浴露
day cream 日霜	night cream 晚霜
eye gel 眼部凝胶	facial mask/masque 面膜
eye mask 眼膜	lip care 护唇用

lip coat 口红护膜	facial scrub 磨砂膏
(deep) pore cleanser/striper pore refining 去黑头	exfoliating scrub 去死皮
body lotion/moisturizer 润肤露（身体）	hand lotion 护手霜

③ 美甲 Manicure

🔵 高频单句大放送

01. Let's go shopping for some beautiful nail stickers.
我们去买一些漂亮的指甲贴吧。

02. How can I keep my nail polish lasting longer?
我怎么才能让指甲油保持时间长一些?

03. There are many nail care products on the market at present.
目前市场上有很多指甲保养的产品。

04. I want my cuticles cut, please.
请帮我修剪一下指甲周围的表皮。

05. I'd like to get a pedicure.
我想修理脚趾甲。

06. How long will it take to make my nails dry?
把指甲弄干需要多长时间?

07. I'd like to manicure my nails round.
我想把指甲修成圆形的。

08. Use a light nail varnish, please.
请用浅色的指甲油。

09. Some girls varnish their toe nails.
一些女孩子在脚趾甲上涂指甲油。

10. I forget to take off my nail polish with remover.
我忘了用洗甲水除掉指甲油。

🔵 口语问答面对面

Toni: Rita, look at my new nail set. How do you think of it?
Rita: Wow! Very pretty!
托妮: 丽塔，你看我新做的指甲。你觉得怎么样?
丽塔: 哇，很漂亮。

Toni: When did you have your nails manicured?

Rita: Last weekend.

托妮: 你什么时候去修的指甲?

丽塔: 上周末。

Toni: That nail beauty store offers many manicure services.

Rita: Did you do the full service?

托妮: 那家美甲店提供很多修甲服务。

丽塔: 你做的全套服务吗?

Toni: No. I only paint and polish my nails.

Rita: But they told me the full service would make my nails look a lot prettier and it was on discount.

托妮: 没有，我只是做了磨光和上色。

丽塔: 但是她们告诉我全套服务会使我的指甲看起来更漂亮，而且还有折扣呢。

Rita: How did they manicure your nails?

Toni: First the nail specialist repaired my nails, and then she let me choose the nail polish. They have a selection of colors. It was hard for me to choose, so the nail specialist helped me.

丽塔: 她们是怎么给你美甲的?

托妮: 她们先是给我修理指甲，然后让我挑一种指甲油。她们那里有很多种颜色可选。对我来说，选个颜色有点难，所以那个美甲师就帮我选了。

Rita: Oh, this color suits you well.

Toni: Yes, I am satisfied with it. Furthermore, the nail specialist is very kind to others.

丽塔: 哦，这个颜色挺适合你的。

托妮: 是呀，我很满意。还有，那个美甲师对人非常和善。

Rita: Next time when I want to get a manicure, you can recommend her to me.

Toni: No problem.

丽塔: 下次我去美甲时，你可以把她推荐给我。

托妮: 没问题。

Rita: Eighty yuan for once. If I buy their card for ten times, they will give a 10% discount.

Toni: I also think it is too expensive.

丽塔: 一次要 80 元。买一张 10 次的卡，她们会打九折。
托妮: 我也觉得有些贵。

情景单词快记忆

fingernail 指甲	nail remover 指甲拔出器
nail whitening pencil 指甲白色修正笔	nail maintenance/nail care 指甲保养
nail care products 指甲保养品	nail fringe 指甲边缘
nail surface 指甲表面	nail length 指甲长度
nail file 指甲锉刀	nail-splitting scissors 指甲分割剪刀
cuticle 指甲根部表皮	nail lightener 指甲光亮剂
nail polish 指甲油	nail pink 指甲红
nail extension 指甲加长	nail scissors 指甲剪
tip glue 指甲胶	luminescent nail polish 指甲亮光油
nail fashion 指甲流行时尚	nail cosmetology 指甲美容
uneven nail surface 指甲面不平	nail matrix 指甲模型
nail polisher 指甲磨光器	nail bleaching agent 指甲漂白剂
nail edge cutter/nail pliers 指甲钳	nail hardener/nail strengthener 指甲强化剂
nail excision 指甲去除	cuticle softener 指甲柔软器
nail lotion 指甲护理乳液	nail design 指甲样式设计

读书笔记

09 理财 Financial Management

① 收入 Income

🌐 高频单句大放送

01. Your monthly gross salary will increase by 300 yuan.
你每月的总收入会涨 300 元。

02. Do you know the total income per month of your family?
你知道你的家庭月总收入吗？

03. His income can't support the whole family.
他的收入无法养活家庭。

04. He was born in a low-income family.
他出生于一个低收入家庭。

05. The main income of the family comes from planting crops.
这个家庭的主要收入来源于种庄稼。

06. It is a well-off village.
这是一个小康村。

07. She comes from a middle-income family.
她来自于一个中等收入家庭。

08. The low income brings her a lot of burden.
较低的收入给她带来了不少负担。

09. It is a large income job.
这是一个高收入职业。

10. They don't have fixed income.
他们没有固定的收入。

🌐 口语问答面对面

Falcon: How time flies! It's pay day again!
Mike: Yes, it is!
福尔肯: 时间过得真快！又到发薪日了！
迈克: 是呀，真快！

Mike: You're an engineer, aren't you?

Falcon: Yes, I am.

迈克: 你是工程师，是吗？

福尔肯: 是的。

Mike: So you must be earning decently, don't you?

Falcon: Well, just average.

迈克: 那你钱一定挣得不少喽？

福尔肯: 哦，只不过一般而已。

Mike: What's your salary then, may I ask?

Falcon: Sure. My monthly pay is $2,500.

迈克: 那能不能问一下你的薪水是多少？

福尔肯: 当然，我每月的工资是 2500 美元。

Falcon: What about yours?

Mike: I'm paid weekly, and it's around $700 per week.

福尔肯: 你的呢？

迈克: 我拿的是周薪，每星期大约 700 美元。

Falcon: That means you can get $2,800 a month, right? That's quite a sum of money.

Mike: Yes, but my pay is on an hourly basis and it's not up to much.

福尔肯: 那就是说你每月可得 2800 美元，对吗？这是相当可观的一笔钱呢！

迈克: 是的，不过我的工资是以小时计算的，而这笔收入并不那么多。

Falcon: Then you must be working overtime.

Mike: That's right. I work 24 hours overtime a week. And the overtime pay is usually more than the regular pay.

福尔肯: 那么你一定在加班工作了。

迈克: 对，我一星期加班 24 小时。而加班工资通常要高于固定工资。

Falcon: So overtime has a bearing on how much you may make in a job. Don't you think so?

Mike: Definitely. And the degree of responsibility in a job also has a great deal to do with the salary.

福尔肯: 所以加班影响工资收入的多少，你不这样认为吗？

迈克: 是这样，而且工作中所负责任的轻重程度同薪水也有密切联系。

Mike: So are other factors such as experience and fringe benefits.

Falcon: No doubt about that. But anyway I have to work hard to earn my money.

迈克：是的，其他如经验、福利待遇等因素也是这样。

福尔肯：没错。但不管怎么说我得努力工作才能赚到钱。

Falcon: Do you know the total income per month of your family?

Mike: Yes, of course.

福尔肯：你知道你的家庭月总收入吗？

迈克：是的，当然了。

情景单词快记忆

pay check 工资支票	pay stub 工资存根
pay period 工资周期	pay rate 工资标准
gross 总额	salary 薪水
wage 时薪	piece wage 计件工资
commission 佣金	bonuse 奖金
deduction 扣除	income tax 个人所得税
pension 养老金	medical insurance 医疗保险
net wage 净工资	raise 加薪
direct deposit 直接存入银行	decently 体面地
average 平均	pay day 发薪日

② 支出 Expenditure

高频单句大放送

01. He can only maintain the daily expenditure reluctantly.
他仅能勉强维持日常开支。

02. The overhead costs are ridiculously expensive.
日常开支太高了。

03. Expenditures by the Federal Government have been steadily pared.
联邦政府的开支正在逐渐削减。

04. An announcement of further cuts in government expenditure is imminent.
最近将发布进一步削减政府开支的公告。

05. The expenditure of money on clothing is very large.
购置衣物的开支很大。

06. We intend to cut expenditure on travelling.
我们打算削减旅行开支。

07. Do you know your total expenditure of the whole year?
你们计算过你们的全年开支吗?

08. If you want to cut down your daily expenditure, you'd better throw away your credit card.
如果你想减少日常开支,你最好扔掉信用卡。

09. Our cost is too high to our endurance.
我们的花销超出了我们的承受能力。

10. This month we need to do a budget.
这个月我们需要做个预算。

口语问答面对面

A: Welcome Mr. and Mrs. Carnwell, please take a seat.
B: Thank you.
A: 欢迎康沃尔夫妇,请坐。
B: 谢谢。

A: So I understand that your family spending has skyrocketed and you want to start budgeting.
C: Yes, that's correct. Frankly speaking, our house-hold income is relatively high and we have never had any money problems, but I think this is the main reason as to why our spending has gone out of control.
A: 那么我了解到了你们的家庭支出在飞涨,于是从现在起你们打算要做个预算。
C: 是的,你说的没错。一般来讲我们的家庭收入算是相对较高的了,我们从来没有任何财政问题,但我认为这就是为什么我们的支出会超出控制的主要原因。

A: I need you to bring all of your receipts for the last two to three months. In that way, we can determine what your average expenditures are and see which category you are spending money on the most. Usually, your fixed costs are higher and we can't do much about that, but we can usually trim your variable costs such as entertainment or clothing.
C: Great! We will do that then!
A: 我需要你们把上两三个月的所有收据都带来。那样的话,我们就可以确认一下你们的平均支出并看看你们哪一项的花销最多。通常来说，你们的固定花销比较高，我们对此也束手无策，但是通常我们可以削减你们的可变花销，例如娱乐和服装。

C: 太好了! 我们会按照那样做的!

B: Now how about we treat you to a nice dinner?

A: That's another thing. If you really want to stop spending so much money, throw away at least half of your credit cards!

B: 那么现在我们请你吃顿饭怎么样?

A: 那是另一码事。如果你们真的想终止高额的花销，至少要扔掉你们一半的信用卡。

A: First what we need to do is to determine your cash flow. Knowing how much money is coming in will help us allocate spending to different categories such as mortgage, education, groceries, etc.

B: Yes, that makes sense.

A: 我们首先要做的是确认一下你们现在的流动资金。知道有多少钱可以帮助你们分配在不同物品的花销上，如房款、教育、生活用品等。

B: 是的，你说的有道理。

A: Do you know your total expenditure of the whole year?

B: Never.

A: 你们计算过你们的全年开支吗?

B: 从来没有计算过。

情景单词快记忆

lend 贷出	lender 贷款人；借出人；放款人
lending 贷款；放款	lending agreement 借贷协议
lessee 承租人	lessor 出租人；批租人
letter of assurance 保证书	letter of confirmation 证实书；确认书
letter of guarantee 保证书	letter of intent 意向书
levy 征费；征款	liability 负债；法律责任
licence 许可证；牌照；特许文件	licence fee 牌照费
licensed bank 持牌银行	licensed intermediary 持牌中介团体
licensed trader 持牌买卖商	lien 留置权；扣押权

life assurance 人寿保险	life assurance policy 人寿保单
life insurance fund 人寿保险基金	life interest 终身权益
life-long product 终身产品	loan fund 贷款基金
loan interest 贷款利息	loan officer 贷款人员
loan repayment 贷款还款	loan shark 高利贷者
local branch 本地分行	local cost 本地成本

③ 买车 Buying a Car

🔵 高频单句大放送

01. Why not try this car?
为什么不试试这辆车？

02. Is $10,000 a good price for a car?
一万美元买辆车是个好价钱吗？

03. Will you offer any discount right now?
你们现在有什么折扣吗？

04. Where can I find a good deal on a vehicle?
我在哪里买车比较合算？

05. What kind of car is safe?
哪种车更安全？

06. Could you tell us more about its standard features?
你能告诉我更多有关这车的标准配置吗？

07. Do you know if this car gets good miles per gallon?
你知道这辆车每加仑跑得多远吗？

08. It's still in the holiday sale and I'll give you a real deal at 10 thousand dollars.
现在还是节假日促销，我给你一个最便宜的价，一万元。

09. What are the miles per gallon like on this car?
这车每加仑油能跑多少英里？

10. What's the safest car out there?
最安全的车是哪种？

🔵 口语问答面对面

Salesman: May I help you?
Jack: Yeah. I come here for a sports car.

业务员: 我能帮您吗?

杰克: 是的。我来这里买辆跑车。

Jack: What kind of car is safe?

Salesman: I think a car with full-automatic transmission is safe.

杰克: 哪种车比较安全?

业务员: 我觉得全自动挡的车比较安全。

Jack: I like the automatic transmission.

Salesman: Look at this car. You can have a test drive.

杰克: 我喜欢自动换挡的。

业务员: 看看这辆车, 你可以试车。

Jack: Could you tell us more about its standard features?

Salesman: Here's a brochure. Get in the car and I will show you.

杰克: 你能告诉我们更多有关这车的标准配置吗?

业务员: 这里有宣传单。上车来我给你们展示一下。

Jack: What we really need is a compact car for our family.

Salesman: If you want comfort and utility, this one is for you.

杰克: 我们需要的是一辆家用小型车。

业务员: 如果你们想要舒适实用的话, 这一款车适合你们。

Jack: I'm in the market for a new car.

Salesman: Do you like this one? I think it is just the one for you.

杰克: 我想在车市买辆新车。

业务员: 你喜欢这辆吗? 我觉得这辆车很适合你的。

Jack: What is the gas mileage?

Salesman: A quarter will go for a mile.

杰克: 油耗是多少?

业务员: 跑一英里只需要消耗 0.25 美元的油。

Jack: Great! Do you have a black one?

Salesman: Yes. This way, please.

杰克: 好极了! 你们有黑色的吗?

业务员: 有, 这边请。

Jack: OK. How much is it?

Salesman: 10 thousand dollars.

杰克: 好的。多少钱？

业务员: 一万美元。

Jack: How about 9.7 thousand dollars? I'll pay in cash.

Salesman: You're a real killer at bargaining. I'll hand that to you. Follow me please.

杰克: 9700 美元怎么样？我付现金。

业务员: 你可真是会杀价。卖给你了，请跟我来。

🔵 情景单词快记忆

Volkswagen 大众	Bugatti 布加蒂
Seat 西雅特	Ferrari 法拉利
Fiat 菲亚特	Maserati 玛莎拉蒂
Lancia 蓝旗亚	Toyota 丰田
Lexus 雷克萨斯	Scion 赛恩
Daihatsu 大发	Renault 雷诺
Infiniti 英菲尼迪	Nissan 尼桑
Hummer 悍马	Pontiac 庞蒂克
Buick 别克	Chevrolet 雪佛兰
Cadillac 凯迪拉克	Suzuki 铃木
Opel 欧宝	Saab 萨博
Subaru 斯巴鲁	Saturn 土星
Holden 霍顿	Daewoo 大宇
Rover 罗孚	Volvo 沃尔沃
Ford 福特	Lincoln 林肯
Mazda 马自达	Jaguar 捷豹
Skoda 斯柯达	

10 邂逅爱情 Falling in Love

① 一见钟情 Love at the First Sight

🔵 高频单句大放送

01. I have fallen in love with him.
我已经爱上他了。

02. He loves her crazily.
他疯狂地爱她。

03. His girlfriend is a knockout!
他的女朋友很迷人!

04. Sally's boyfriend was really a heartbreaker.
萨利的男朋友很帅。

05. The man asked me out last night but I refused.
那个男人昨晚约我出去但是被我拒绝了。

06. Jackie Chan really turns me on.
成龙让我很着迷。

07. Sally is really elegant, so many boys are lusting after her.
萨利真的很优雅,所以很多男孩子追求她。

08. David will make a pass at her.
大卫要追求她。

09. I feel the boy is infatuated with you.
我觉得那个男孩对你有意思。

10. Recently, many boys have made advances to her.
最近,很多男孩子向她求爱。

🔵 口语问答面对面

Tina: Hi, Sally. Who was the boy with you just now?
Sally: Well, he is my boyfriend. I've decided to go steady with him.
蒂娜:嗨,萨利。刚刚和你一起的男孩是谁啊?
萨利:哦,他是我男朋友。我已经决定和他交往了。

Tina: You're quite sure he's your Mr. Right?

Sally: Yes. He's the just person I had dreamed of.

蒂娜: 那么，你确信他就是你想找的那个人？

萨利: 是的。他就是我一直梦想着要找的人。

Tina: Can you tell me something about him? Such as what type of man he is?

Sally: In my eyes, he's a mature, stable, manly one.

蒂娜: 你能告诉我关于他的一些事吗？比如他是哪种类型的人？

萨利: 在我眼里，他是一个成熟、踏实、阳刚的男子。

Sally: I believe someday I'll marry him.

Tina: Sounds nice! Congratulations for you find your ideal partner.

萨利: 我相信有一天我要嫁给他。

蒂娜: 听起来不错！恭喜你找到了理想的另一半。

Tina: I can feel you're serious this time. May you happy!

Sally: Thank you.

蒂娜: 我能感觉到你这次是认真的。祝你幸福！

萨利: 谢谢。

Sally: But why don't you find a boyfriend now? You know most of the people at the same age of us all have friends.

Tina: Yes, you're right. But I still can't meet the right boy. To tell the truth I often feel lonely when I'm free.

萨利: 但是你现在为什么不找个男朋友呢？要知道和我们同龄的人大部分都有对象了啊。

蒂娜: 是啊，你说得对。但是我始终没有遇到合适的男孩。说实话，当我闲下来时经常觉得很孤独。

Sally: Come on. Don't worry, you're so nice and feminine. You'll meet a good boy who really loves you someday.

Tina: Thank you, I hope so.

萨利: 没事的。别急，你是那么漂亮温柔的女孩。总有一天你会遇见真正爱你的男孩的。

蒂娜: 谢谢，希望如此。

Sally: I feel the boy is infatuated with you.

Tina: I don't think so.

萨利: 我觉得那个男孩对你有意思。
蒂娜: 我不这么认为。

情景单词快记忆

to call on 拜访	to be engaged 约会
engagement 约会；约定	play hard-to-get 欲擒故纵
have a crush on 迷恋	stand someone up 放某人鸽子
go steady with sb. 与某人交往	hook up connection 介绍；认识
hook up 介绍	babe 对年轻女子或爱人的昵称
break up 分手	fine 美好的
happy 幸福的	wonderful 极好的
shy 害羞的	proud 骄傲的
optimistic 积极的	satisfied 满意的

② 表达爱意 Expressing Love

高频单句大放送

01. I would like to talk with you.
    我想和你谈谈。

02. Have you got a girlfriend?
    你有女朋友吗?

03. I fell in love with you the moment I saw you.
    见到你的那一刻我就爱上了你。

04. How do you like me?
    你感觉我这个人怎样?

05. I am thinking of you day and night.
    我日日夜夜都在想着你。

06. You are the whole world for me.
    对于我来说你就是整个世界。

07. I can't live without you.
    没有你我不能活。

08. I'd like to live the rest of my life with you.
我想和你共度余生。

09. Your mature personality attracts me deeply.
你成熟的个性深深地吸引了我。

10. I would keep you company all my life.
我愿意伴你一生。

口语问答面对面

Tom: How time flies. How was your weekend going ?
Lillian: I had a great time. I went climbing the Great Wall with my sisters. And we also had a picnic.
汤姆: 时间飞快，周末过得怎样？
莉莲: 我玩得很开心。我和姐妹一起去爬长城了。我们还举行了野餐。

Tom: I regret not joining you.
Lillian: I will call you next time.
汤姆: 真后悔没有加入你们。
莉莲: 下次我会叫上你。

Lillian: Will you see the photos we took that day?
Tom: Certainly.
莉莲: 想要看看我们那天拍的照片吗？
汤姆: 当然了。

Tom: Who is this girl?
Lillian: She is Jane, my little sister.
汤姆: 这个女孩是谁呀？
莉莲: 她是简，我的妹妹。

Lillian: She is attractive, isn't she?
Tom: In my mind, you are the most beautiful girl in the world.
莉莲: 她很有魅力，对吧？
汤姆: 在我看来，你是世界上最漂亮的女孩。

Tom: I fell in love with you the moment I saw you. A day without you is like a day without sunshine.
Lillian: Oh, my God.
汤姆: 从看到你的那刻起我就爱上了你。没有你的日子就如同没有阳光一样。

莉莲: 天哪。

Tom: How do you like me ?
Lillian: I regard you as sincere, brave, hardworking...In a word, you are an excellent man.
汤姆: 你是怎么看我的?
莉莲: 你真诚、勇敢、勤劳……总之，你是一个很优秀的人。

Tom: Let me take care of you all my life.
Lillian: I'm sorry, but I think we'd better be friends.
汤姆: 就让我照顾你一辈子吧。
莉莲: 很抱歉，我们还是做朋友吧。

Tom: You know I can't live without you.
Lillian: In fact I have had a lover.
汤姆: 你知道没有你我不能活。
莉莲: 实际上，我已经有了喜欢的人。

情景单词快记忆

puppy love/first love 初恋	love at the first sight 一见钟情
the chemical feeling 触电般的感觉	cute meet 浪漫的邂逅
true love 真爱	courtship 求爱
propose 求婚	a doomed couple 天生一对
promise/pledge/vow 誓言	candlelight dinner 烛光晚餐
a happy ending 大团圆结局	

3 恋爱 Being in Love

高频单句大放送

01. I feel lucky to know you.
认识你我感觉很幸运。

02. I'm so lucky to have you in my life.
我的生命里有你是多么幸运。

03. Seeing you always makes me happy.
看到你总让我很快乐。

04. I feel blessed to have you in my life.
生命里有你我感觉很幸福。

05. You exactly know how to make me happy.
你很清楚怎样使我快乐。

06. You always make my heart beat faster.
你总是让我的心跳加速。

07. I love you.
我爱你。

08. My heart beats so fast when I'm around you.
当我在你身边的时候，我的心跳是如此之快。

09. I have something important to talk to you.
我有些重要的事情要跟你说。

10. I really like this girl. I think I love her.
我真的喜欢这个女孩，我想我爱上她了。

口语问答面对面

A: I love you.
B: I love you, too.
A: 我爱你。
B: 我也爱你。

A: You really turn me on.
B: I'm sorry, I'm not sure I feel the same about you.
A: 你真的让我神魂颠倒。
B: 抱歉，我不确定我的感觉和你的一样。

A: What do you think of me?
B: You're my type.
A: 你觉得我怎么样?
B: 你是我喜欢的类型。

A: I have a hunch that Linda likes me.
B: Are you sure?
A: 我有一种感觉琳达喜欢我。
B: 你确定?

A: Seeing you always makes me happy.

B: You make me happy, too.

A: 看到你总让我很快乐。

B: 你也让我很快乐。

A: If I want to hold your hands, will you say yes?

B: Yes, I love you.

A: 如果我想牵你的手，你会同意吗?

B: 会，我爱你。

A: I think I'm in love.

B: That's so sweet.

A: 我想我恋爱了。

B: 那太好了。

读书笔记

11 关于爱情
About Love

① 吵架 Quarreling

🔵 高频单句大放送

01. You are always cheating on me.
    你一直在欺骗我。

02. I regret having met you.
    我后悔遇见了你。

03. You will drive me mad.
    你要把我逼疯了。

04. You are a selfish man.
    你是一个自私的人。

05. I don't want to stay with you any longer.
    我再也不想跟你在一起了。

06. You have broken my heart.
    你已经伤透了我的心。

07. I can't stand you any more.
    我受不了你了。

08. I need more freedom.
    我需要更多的自由。

09. Maybe we should keep calm and have a talk.
    也许我们应该平静一下好好谈谈。

10. Leave me alone.
    让我自己待会儿。

🔵 口语问答面对面

Lillian: I can't stand you any more. I'm tired of your smoking.
Jack: I promise to give up.
莉莲: 我再也受不了你了。我讨厌你抽烟。
杰克: 我保证戒掉。

Jack: Give me a chance!

Lillian: I forget how many chances I have given you.

杰克: 给我一次机会!

莉莲: 我已经不记得给过你多少机会了。

Jack: Give me the last chance, darling.

Lillian: Don't call me like this. You treat me so indifferent.

杰克: 给我最后一次机会吧，亲爱的。

莉莲: 不要这么称呼我。你对我这么的冷漠。

Jack: I am just devoted to my career.

Lillian: However, you shouldn't make me lonely.

杰克: 我只是专心于我的事业而已。

莉莲: 无论如何你都不应该让我感到寂寞。

Jack: That's because I want to make more money. I want you to live a better life.

Lillian: I wouldn't listen to your explanation.

杰克: 那是因为我想要挣更多的钱，我想让你过上好的生活。

莉莲: 我不要听你的解释。

Jack: My honey, I promise to spare more time to stay with you.

Lillian: I wouldn't trust you.

杰克: 亲爱的，我保证多抽出时间来陪你。

莉莲: 我不相信你了。

Lillian: I can't stand you any more.

Jack: Don't treat me like this. I need your love.

莉莲: 我受不了你了。

杰克: 不要这么对我。我需要你的爱。

Lillian: You are always cheating on me.

Jack: Maybe we should keep calm and have a talk.

莉莲: 你一直在欺骗我。

杰克: 也许我们应该平静一下好好谈谈。

Lillian: You have broken my heart.

Jack: I'm sorry.

莉莲: 你已经伤透了我的心。

杰克: 很抱歉。

Lillian: I regret having met you.
Jack: So do I.
莉莲: 我后悔遇见了你。
杰克: 我也是。

🔵 情景单词快记忆

stupid 愚蠢的	freak 怪人
dirty old man 老色鬼	shoddy 奸诈的；卑鄙的
shrew 泼妇；悍妇	blockhead 傻瓜
a woman of great beauty 大美人	charlatan 骗子
charlie 蠢人；傻瓜	chatterbox 话匣子；话多的人
mobster 匪徒；犯罪分子	monkey business 欺骗；恶作剧
lunatic 严重精神病患者	lustful 好色的
nonsense 胡说；胡闹	careless 粗心的

② 分手 Breaking Up

🔵 高频单句大放送

01. Things have changed. I think we need to talk.
一切都变了，我们需要谈谈。

02. I'm not sure we are working out.
我不确定我们正在解决。

03. We've been fighting a lot recently.
我们最近总是吵架。

04. It's nothing against you, our relationship just isn't going smoothly anymore.
这不关你的事，只是我们的关系不再那么顺畅了。

05. I still like you as a person. Can we remain friends?
我还是挺喜欢你这个人的。我们还能做朋友吗？

06. I really think we should break up.
我真的觉得我们应该分手了。

07. I don't think we should stay friends.
我觉得我们不应该保持朋友关系。

08. I don't think we should see each other anymore.
我觉得我们彼此还是不要再见了。

09. I want to stay friends…can't we at least try?
我还想做朋友……难道我们不能再试一下吗？

10. Are you just giving up?
你难道要放弃吗？

口语问答面对面

Lucy: We need to talk.

Jack: What is it?

露西: 我们需要谈谈。

杰克: 什么事呀？

Lucy: We have been fighting too much lately. All I do seems to make you sad.

Jack: Yeah, I know. We used to be happy, but lately we have been making each other depressed.

露西: 我们最近总是吵架。我所做的好像只是让你心烦。

杰克: 是啊，我明白。我们曾经是那么快乐，但最近我们总是一直让对方郁闷。

Lucy: That's why I think we should break up.

Jack: I knew you would say that…and I agree.

露西: 那就是我觉得我们应该分手的原因。

杰克: 我就知道你会那么说……我同意。

Lucy: I just don't think we could ever go back to that.We have been through too much.

Jack: I know.

露西: 我只是觉得我们再也回不到以前那样了，我们经历得太多了。

杰克: 我明白。

Jack: So are we going to stay friends?

Lucy: I'd like that, but if you need a break-up, I'll understand. You're still important to me.

杰克: 那我们还是朋友吗？

露西: 我很愿意，但如果你要和我断绝关系我也会理解的。你对我仍然很重要。

Jack: We can try to stay friends.

Lucy: Thanks.

杰克: 我们可以试着做朋友。
露西: 谢谢。

Lucy: I'm sorry about all this.
Jack: It's alright. I know this is for the best.
露西: 我对这一切很抱歉。
杰克: 没关系，我知道这是最好的办法。

Jack: But I really miss how we used to be.
Lucy: Me too.
杰克: 但是我真的怀念以前的日子。
露西: 我也是。

情景单词快记忆

one-sided love 单相思	lose one's love 失恋
fancy sick 害相思病的	love token 定情信物
love letter 情书	lover's vows 山盟海誓
court 求爱	

③ 拒绝求婚 Refusing Proposal

高频单句大放送

01. I don't want to get married.
    我还不想结婚。

02. I would like not to rush into marriage.
    我不想这么快就结婚。

03. We have little in common.
    我们共同语言太少了。

04. I think marriage will affect my career.
    我觉得婚姻会影响我的事业。

05. I wouldn't marry a man like you.
    我不想嫁给一个你这样的人。

06. We wouldn't be happy if we get married.
    我们结婚的话不会幸福的。

07. I wouldn't get married at so early age.
我不想这么早结婚。

08. I think marriage will damage our love.
我觉得婚姻会破坏我们的爱情。

09. I am not going to marry a poor man.
我不打算嫁给一个穷光蛋。

10. I will marry you the day you get mature.
等你成熟的那天我就嫁给你。

口语问答面对面

Jack: How do you like me?
Lillian: I regard you as a honest, hardworking, kind man.
杰克: 你觉得我怎样?
莉莲: 你诚实、努力并且很有爱心。

Jack: I'd like to ask you a question if you don't mind.
Lillian: Go ahead, please.
杰克: 如果你不介意的话，我想问你一个问题。
莉莲: 请讲。

Jack: Will you marry me?
Lillian: It's so unexpected.
杰克: 嫁给我好吗?
莉莲: 太突然了。

Jack: I have thought about it for several months. I expect to live with you.
Lillian: You are just the best friend in my mind.
杰克: 我已经考虑了几个月了。我想要跟你一起生活。
莉莲: 在我心里你只是最好的朋友。

Jack: Why can't we become couples?
Lillian: We are too familiar with each other.
杰克: 为什么我们不能成为夫妻呢?
莉莲: 我们太熟悉彼此了。

Jack: Will you marry me?
Lillian: I would like not to rush into marriage.
杰克: 嫁给我好吗?

莉莲: 我不想这么快就结婚。

Jack: Will you be my wife?
Lillian: I wouldn't marry a man like you.
杰克: 做我的妻子好吗?
莉莲: 我不想嫁给一个你这样的人。

Jack: Let's tie the knot!
Lillian: No, I can't marry you. I'm sorry.
杰克: 咱们结婚吧!
莉莲: 不, 我不能跟你结婚, 对不起。

Jack: Let's tie the knot!
Lillian: I wouldn't get married at so early age.
杰克: 咱们结婚吧!
莉莲: 我不想这么早结婚。

Lillian: Please forgive me, my friends.
Jack: It doesn't matter.
莉莲: 请原谅我, 朋友。
杰克: 没关系的。

🔵 情景单词快记忆

marriage 婚姻	career 事业
damage 破坏	mature 成熟的
unexpected 意外的	tie the knot 结婚
chained 受束缚的	rush into 匆忙
against my will 违背我的意愿	do me not good 对我没什么好处
concentrate on my work 集中精力工作	

读书笔记

幸福时刻
Happy Moment

① 闪婚 Flash Marriage

高频单句大放送

01. We haven't been dating too long, but I really like her.
我们约会还没多长时间，但我真的喜欢她。

02. I want us to get married.
我想我们应该结婚了。

03. My girlfriend and I are doing great.
我和我女朋友相处得很好。

04. Don't you think it's too early for saying that kind of stuff?
你不觉得这么说有点早了吗?

05. Let's have our wedding in Las Vegas. They have last minute ceremonies there.
咱们在拉斯维加斯举行婚礼吧，他们有快速婚礼。

06. It's pretty early, but if you think it's true love, I don't see why not.
太早了，但如果你觉得是真正的爱情，那我还有什么不可以的呢?

07. Our wedding in Las Vegas was so awesome!
我们在拉斯维加斯的婚礼真是太棒了!

08. Vegas is amazing, and our wedding went so well for a last minute thing.
拉斯维加斯太棒了，我们的整个婚礼进行得都很顺利。

09. That's great. I hope you two are happy together.
挺好的，希望你们俩在一起幸福。

10. We should go to Las Vegas for our wedding, since we want to get married soon and everything is done.
我们应该去拉斯维加斯举行婚礼，因为我们想马上结婚而且一切都准备妥当。

口语问答面对面

Jason: Hey! Do you remember that girl called Lillian I told you about?
Paul: Yeah. You two have been dating, right?
詹森: 嘿! 你还记得上次我跟你说的那个叫莉莲的女孩吗?

保罗: 是的。你们俩一直在约会吗?

Jason: My girlfriend and I are doing great.

Paul: Awesome, I'm happy for you.

詹森: 我和我女朋友相处得很好。

保罗: 太好了, 我为你们感到高兴。

Jason: Your lightning marriage freaked out a bunch of people.

Paul: I think so. We were in a hurry to get married then.

詹森: 你们的闪婚真是吓坏了不少人。

保罗: 我想是吧, 当时我们都着急结婚。

Jason: We felt sparks as soon as we met. I have a hunch that she's the one.

Paul: You think you have fallen in love with her already?

詹森: 我们一见钟情, 我有预感她就是我要找的人。

保罗: 你觉得你已经爱上她了?

Jason: We only met three months ago, and now we're married.

Paul: Ah, this flash marriage is really becoming a thing.

詹森: 我们刚刚认识 3 个月就结婚了。

保罗: 哇, 闪婚真是变得流行起来了。

Jason: Donna and I are getting married.

Paul: Married? Didn't you just meet her a few months ago?

詹森: 唐娜和我要结婚了。

保罗: 结婚? 你不是才认识她几个月吗?

Paul: What do you mean, bro?

Jason: Lillian and I are getting married.

保罗: 兄弟, 你什么意思?

詹森: 莉莲和我要准备结婚了!

Paul: Married? Didn't you just meet her a few months ago?

Jason: Yeah, but we've become really close. I think we're going to Las Vegas to get married in one of those drive-thru weddings.

保罗: 结婚? 你不是才认识她几个月吗?

詹森: 是啊, 但是我们已经很亲密了。我们打算在拉斯维加斯举行快速婚礼。

Paul: Well man, I can't say I agree with your decision, but just do what makes you happy.

Jason: Thanks for the support. Lillian makes me happy, and I can't wait until we get married.

保罗: 哦，哥们儿，虽然我不认同你的决定，但是只要你开心就好。

詹森: 谢谢你的支持。莉莲让我很开心，我都迫不及待想要跟她结婚了。

Paul: Yeah, I can see that. I really hope you two are great together.

Jason: Thanks, man! I'll send you pictures of the ceremony!

保罗: 是啊，我能看出来。我希望你们俩在一起幸福。

詹森: 谢谢，哥们儿! 我会给你送婚礼照片的!

情景单词快记忆

speed dating 闪电约会	whirlwind romance 闪电恋爱
flash marriage 闪电结婚	wedding slave 婚奴
mortgage slave 房奴	quick pregnancy 闪孕
marriage certificate 结婚证	fiance 未婚夫
fiancee 未婚妻	bridal chamber 新房
trial marriage 试婚	early marriage 早婚
late marriage 晚婚	remarriage 再婚
wedding planning 婚庆策划	wedding guest 婚庆来客
wedding party 婚礼晚会	wedding gift 贺礼
dowry 嫁妆	bridal hairstyle 新娘发型

② 婚礼 Wedding

高频单句大放送

01. Do you want to get our families together to discuss wedding plan?
你想把咱们家里人召集在一起讨论一下婚礼的安排吗?

02. Where do you want the wedding to be?
你希望婚礼在哪里举行?

03. Did you make an appointment with the wedding planner?
你和婚礼策划师约好了吗?

04. Who do you want to send our invitations to?
你都想给谁发请帖?

05. Did you buy your dress yet?
    你买结婚礼服了吗?

06. Do you want to pick out a catering service today?
    你今天想挑选餐饮服务吗?

07. What kind of food do you want for the wedding?
    婚礼上你想要什么食物?

08. Let's plan out the honeymoon.
    咱们计划一下蜜月吧。

09. Thanks for the wedding gifts, everyone!
    谢谢大家的礼物!

10. It's great to see you tie the knot.
    看到你们喜结连理真好。

口语问答面对面

Lillian: Hey! I want your opinion on something.
Jack: What is it?
莉莲: 嘿! 有些事情问问你的意见。
杰克: 什么事?

Lillian: I want the wedding to be perfect. Let's discuss it whenever you want.
Jack: We don't have to have an elaborate wedding.
莉莲: 我想让这个婚礼很完美,你什么时候想的话咱们就讨论一下吧。
杰克: 我们不必要办一个这么煞费苦心的婚礼。

Lillian: I have been thinking about the colors for the wedding today and I wanted to ask you about them.
Jack: Alright, shoot.
莉莲: 我一直在想婚礼的色彩,我想问一下你对此有什么意见。
杰克: 好的,说吧。

Lillian: I was thinking we should do a white and baby blue color scheme, but now I think I would like a sea-foam green color with the white. What do you think?
Jack: I want whatever you want.
莉莲: 我原计划是白色和蓝色,但现在我觉得海泡绿和白色搭配更好。你觉得呢?
杰克: 你想要什么颜色我都喜欢。

Lillian: But I can't decide by myself! Which color do you like better?

Jack: Well, if you're having trouble, why don't you pick out your flowers first and base the color around that?

莉莲: 但是我自己没法决定! 你更喜欢什么颜色?

杰克: 如果你难以决定的话为什么不先挑选花, 在花的颜色的基础上再决定呢?

Lillian: Oh, that's a pretty good idea, sweetie. Thanks! I think I'll go with the green then. Green will go with any flower.

Jack: Sounds great to me.

莉莲: 哦, 这是个不错的主意。谢谢! 我想到时候我会用绿色搭配, 绿色和任何花都相配。

杰克: 听起来不错。

Lillian: Have you found a dress that you like?

Jack: I didn't find a dress I liked, so my friend and I are going out again today to look for one.

莉莲: 你找到你喜欢的礼服了吗?

杰克: 我还没有找到一件我喜欢的礼服, 所以我朋友他们和我打算今天再出去找一件。

Jack: Do you want to talk about the honeymoon?

Lillian: Yes! I know exactly where I want the honeymoon to be.

杰克: 你想谈谈蜜月的事吗?

莉莲: 好啊! 我知道我想去哪里度蜜月。

情景单词快记忆

wedding ceremony 结婚典礼

wedding reception 婚宴

register office 结婚登记处

trousseau 嫁妆

usher 引宾员; 门房; 传达员

vows 婚誓

say one's vows 立下婚誓

wedding day 举行婚礼的日子

wedding anniversary 结婚周年纪念日

pastor 牧师

groomsman 伴郎

bridesmaid 伴娘

honeymoon 蜜月

wedding dress 婚纱; 结婚礼服

wed in a civil ceremony 登记结婚

marriage certificate 结婚证

guest 来宾

marriage after divorce 再婚

bride 新娘	wedding march 婚礼进行曲
bridegroom/groom 新郎	mixed marriage 涉外婚姻；跨国婚姻

③ 婚姻生活 Marriage Life

高频单句大放送

01. We are satisfied with our marriage life.
我们很满意我们的婚姻生活。

02. We should share our happiness and sorrow together.
我们应该一起分享快乐和忧伤。

03. The husband should do the housework together with the wife.
丈夫应该和妻子一起做家务。

04. The wife should show understanding and sympathy to the husband.
妻子应该多多体谅丈夫。

05. They should be responsible for family.
他们应该对自己的婚姻负责。

06. Children can make the marriage life sweet and perfect.
孩子可以使婚姻生活更加的甜蜜完美。

07. There is nothing better than marriage life.
没有什么比婚姻生活更好的了。

08. We should depend on each other.
我们应该互相依靠。

09. We experienced much happiness and sorrow together.
我们一起经历了许多快乐和忧伤。

10. I feel lots of pressure when living with you.
我觉得和你一起生活很压抑。

口语问答面对面

Jack: How do you like the marriage life?
Lillian: It plays an important part in my life.
杰克：你怎样看待婚姻生活？
莉莲：它在我的生活中起着很重要的作用。

Jack: Do you think it good to yourself?
Lillian: That depends on what the marriage life is like.

杰克: 它对你自身而言有好处吗?

莉莲: 那得看是什么样的婚姻了。

Jack: What do you think of "Marriage is the grave of love"?

Lillian: I consider it a misunderstanding of marriage.

杰克: 你怎么理解 "婚姻是爱情的坟墓" ?

莉莲: 我认为那是对婚姻的一种误解。

Jack: How should we make the marriage life happy?

Lillian: We should share happiness and sorrow together. We must understand each other at any time.

杰克: 我们应该怎样使婚姻生活幸福呢?

莉莲: 我们应该共同分享快乐和忧伤。任何时候都要理解彼此。

Jack: What can we do when the quarreling comes?

Lillian: We must keep calm and communicate well. We must pay attention to our attitude.

杰克: 争吵来临时应该怎么做呢?

莉莲: 我们应该保持心态平和并且好好地沟通。一定要注意态度。

Jack: Is there any way to make the marriage life fresh?

Lillian: An unexpected gift will make you feel sweet and fresh. Do celebrate the wedding anniversary. Do have a kid as soon as possible. Kid is the most valuable gift sent to your lover.

杰克: 有没有什么方法使婚姻保鲜呢?

莉莲: 一份意想不到的礼物会使你们感到甜蜜刺激。一定要记得庆祝结婚纪念日。一定记得尽快要个孩子。孩子是送给爱人最珍贵的礼物。

A: Have you ever thought about having children?

B: My parents-in-law want us to have one as soon as possible. But my husband and I decide to wait for a couple of years.

A: 你考虑过要孩子吗?

B: 我公婆想要我们快点生孩子。但是我和我先生决定再等几年。

A: Is it because of your work?

B: Yes, kind of, but that's not the whole story. We thought it's just not the right time and we are not ready to be parents.

A: 是因为工作的关系吗?

B: 是啊，一部分原因吧，也不全是。我想现在不是时候，我们还没准备好做父母。

A: What about you?
B: Well, I've always wanted to have lots of children. Growing up as the only child, I always feel a bit lonely. I want to have two children and my husbands loves kids, too.
A: 你呢？
B: 我一直想要很多孩子。我是独生子，小时候一个人很孤单。我想要两个孩子，我丈夫也很喜欢孩子。

A: Will you have children soon?
B: Maybe next year. You know, we've just bought a car and we need time to save up for the new baby.
A: 你会很快生孩子吗？
B: 也许明年吧。我们刚买了车，需要存点钱为孩子的出生做点准备。

🔵 情景单词快记忆

satisfied 满意的	share 分享
responsible 负责的	sweet and perfect 甜蜜
pressure 压力	depend on each other 相互依靠
misunderstanding 误解	quarrel 争吵
communication 沟通	have a baby 生孩子
a stable marriage 稳固的婚姻	disinterest 不关心
spouse 伴侣	calm 冷静的

读书笔记

13 态度观点
Attitude and Mind

① 喜欢与否 Like and Dislike

高频单句大放送

01. I really like that.
　　我真的喜欢那个。

02. I dislike that.
　　我不喜欢那个。

03. I don't like that.
　　我不喜欢那个。

04. I really don't like that.
　　我真的不喜欢那个。

05. That's awesome.
　　那太棒了。

06. That sucks.
　　那太差劲了。

07. That's awful.
　　那太可怕了。

08. I'm a fan of that.
　　我是它的粉丝。

09. That's cool.
　　那很酷。

10. I hate it.
　　我讨厌它。

口语问答面对面

A: What would you like, tea or coffee?
B: I prefer tea to coffee.
A: 你喜欢什么，茶还是咖啡？
B: 比起咖啡我更喜欢茶。

A: I prefer coffee with sugar.

B: Me too.

A: 我喜欢加糖的咖啡。

B: 我也是。

A: I like that.

B: Me too.

A: 我喜欢那个。

B: 我也是。

A: I'm a fan of it.

B: I don't care for it.

A: 我是那个的粉丝。

B: 我不喜欢。

A: That sucks.

B: You really hate it that much?

A: 那太差劲了。

B: 你真的那么讨厌它吗?

A: I can't stand you.

B: I hate you, too.

A: 我受不了你了。

B: 我也恨你。

A: I dislike that.

B: Really? I love it.

A: 我不喜欢那个。

B: 是吗? 我很喜欢。

A: Egg soup is my cup of tea.

B: Yeah, I know.

A: 我喜欢喝鸡蛋汤。

B: 是啊，我知道的。

A: I've had it.

B: You really hate me that much?

A: 我已经受够了!

B: 你真的那么讨厌我吗?

A: I'm satisfied with this dress.
B: Yeah, it's very beautiful.
A: 我对这件衣服很满意。
B: 是啊，这件衣服很漂亮。

🔵 情景单词快记忆

love 喜欢	like 喜欢
be fond of 喜欢	crazy 狂热的
be crazy about 对……喜欢得发狂	weakness 嗜好
favor 偏爱	be into 对……着迷
enjoy 喜欢	take an interest in 感兴趣
hate 厌恶	dislike 不喜欢
be not interested in 不感兴趣	good for nothing 毫无价值
bear 忍受	messy 混乱的
awful 极坏的	disgusting 让人恶心的
put up with 忍受	

② 同意与否 Agreement and Disagreement

🔵 高频单句大放送

01. I agree with you.
    我同意你的说法。

02. I can't believe you feel that way.
    我不敢相信你是那么想的。

03. I'm glad you think that way.
    我很高兴你会那么认为。

04. I'm surprised we feel the same about it.
    我很吃惊我们对此想法一致。

05. I don't feel the same about it.
    对此，我并不那么认为。

06. I feel the same way.
    我有同感。

07. I thought we would disagree, and I'm surprised that we don't.
我原以为我们会有分歧，没想到竟然没有。

08. That's really cool that you think that way.
你那么想真是太好了。

09. I'm happy you feel that way.
你那么想我很高兴。

10. I agree with your point.
我同意你的观点。

🔵 口语问答面对面

A: As for me, I have no objections about it.
B: It's great that we agree on it.
A: 对我来说，我对此没有反对意见。
B: 我们对此意见一致真是太好了。

A: Don't you agree?
B: I agree with you partially.
A: 你不同意吗?
B: 我部分同意你的观点。

A: I can't agree with everything you said.
B: Let's agree to disagree.
A: 我不完全同意你所说的话。
B: 咱们就求同存异吧。

A: Is that okay?
B: Not on your life!
A: 那样行吗?
B: 绝对不行!

A: I don't feel the same way about it.
B: Oh, that sucks.
A: 对此，我并不那么认为。
B: 哦，那太糟糕了。

A: I feel the same way.
B: Cool.
A: 我有同感。

B: 太好了。

A: What do you think of my proposal?
B: I'm all for it.
A: 你觉得我的建议怎么样?
B: 我非常赞成。

A: I couldn't agree with you more.
B: That sounds okay.
A: 我完全同意你的看法。
B: 那听起来不错。

A: I disagree.
B: Sorry, I thought you would agree.
A: 我不同意。
B: 抱歉, 我以为你会同意的。

A: Do you agree with me about this?
B: Yeah, I agree with you.
A: 关于这一点你同意我的意见吗?
B: 是的, 我同意你的观点。

情景单词快记忆

Fine. 好的。	All right. 好的。
grant 同意	object 反对
work 起作用	Great! 很好!
No way. 不行。	No. 不。
Nope. 不。	No chance. 没有任何可能。
You wish! 你想得倒美!	Not likely. 不可能。
Dream on! 做梦去吧!	Certainly. 当然可以。
You said it. 你说对了。	I said no. 我说过了, 不行的。

③ 信任与怀疑 Trust and Doubt

高频单句大放送

01. I feel like I can't trust you.
我觉得我不能相信你。

02. I don't really want to talk to you about it.
我真的不想跟你说这件事。

03. I want to tell you something, but I'm not sure about it.
我想告诉你一些事情，但我不确定该不该告诉你。

04. I know I can trust you.
我知道我可以信任你。

05. I trust you a lot.
我非常相信你。

06. I'm not sure I can trust you, even though I wish I could.
我不确定我能否相信你，虽然我希望我能。

07. I won't buy your story.
我不相信你说的话。

08. I doubt it.
我怀疑。

09. I think I can trust you.
我想我能相信你。

10. It's chancy.
这不是真的。

口语问答面对面

A: What do you think?
B: I have no doubt about it.
A: 你怎么想？
B: 我对此没什么疑问。

A: I can't prove it. You'll have to take my word for it.
B: I don't buy it.
A: 我无法证明此事，你就相信我好了。
B: 我不相信。

A: Really? Don't you have faith in me?

B: I believe I can trust you.

A: 是吗? 你不相信我吗?

B: 我知道我可以信任你。

A: Why don't you believe me?

B: I believe what you said.

A: 你为什么不相信我呢?

B: 我相信你的话。

A: Do you think she is serious?

B: I trusted her not to go back on her word.

A: 你觉得她是认真的吗?

B: 我相信她不会食言。

A: Are you kidding?

B: I don't think so.

A: 你开玩笑吧?

B: 我不这样认为。

A: Are you joking?

B: No, it's true.

A: 你开玩笑吧?

B: 不，是真的。

A: Why wouldn't you trust me?

B: I take your word for it.

A: 你为什么不相信我呢?

B: 我相信你的话。

A: Do you mean it?

B: Yes, I'm serious.

A: 是真的吗?

B: 是的，我是认真的。

A: Are you serious?

B: No, I'm joking.

A: 你是认真的吗?

B: 不是，我开玩笑的。

情景单词快记忆

confidence 信任；信心；自信	doubt 怀疑
positiveness 确信；自信	doubtful 可疑的；不确的；疑心的
diffidence 缺乏自信	puzzling 迷惑的；莫明其妙的
distrust 不信任；怀疑	negative 否定的；消极的
nonconfidence 不信任；没信心	disapproval 不赞成
confident 有信心的；自信的	objection 异议
confidential 秘密的；机密的；担任机密工作的	opposition 反对
suspicion 猜疑；怀疑	critical 批评的
suspicious 可疑的；怀疑的	criticism 批评批判

读书笔记

第二章

职场商务英语

14 个人信息 Personal Information

① 工作经验 Working Experience

🔵 高频单句大放送

01. Do you have any work experience?
你有工作经验吗？

02. I have some practical experience.
我有一些实际工作经验。

03. What were you responsible for at your previous work?
你原来的工作是负责什么的？

04. What have you learned from jobs you have held?
你从以往的工作中学到了什么？

05. What's your last job?
你上一份工作是做什么的？

06. I have no work experience, but I'm eager to learn.
我没有工作经验，但是我很好学。

07. Have you done some part time job?
你做过兼职吗？

08. How many employers have you worked for?
你曾经为多少个雇主工作过？

09. What position have you had before?
你之前干过什么工作？

10. Would you tell me the essential qualities a secretary should maintain?
你能告诉我一个秘书应该兼具什么素质吗？

🔵 口语问答面对面

(I = interviewer, A = applicant)

I: Have you ever been employed?

A: I worked in a foreign rep office for one year. However, I left there two years ago because the work they gave me was rather dull. I found another job that is more interesting.

面试者: 你以前工作过吗?

求职者: 我以前在一个外国公司代表处工作过一年。然而，因为工作很枯燥，我两年前就离开了。我找到了一个更感兴趣的工作。

I: Have you done any work in this field?

A: Yes, I have learned a lot about business and know how to operate the basic office software.

面试者: 你以前在这一领域干过吗?

求职者: 是的，我学了许多关于商务的知识，知道怎样去操作基本的办公软件。

I: What have you learned from the jobs you have had?

A: I have learned a lot from the former jobs which are related to the job I apply now. Besides I learned at my previous job to cooperate with my colleagues.

面试者: 你从以往的工作中学到了什么?

求职者: 我从以前的工作中学到了很多，并且它们和我现在要申请的工作是相关联的。另外我从以前的工作中还学到要和同事通力合作。

I: What's your major weak point?

A: I haven't been involved in international business too often, so I don't have too much experience.

面试者: 你的主要弱点是什么?

求职者: 我并不是经常涉及国际商务，所以没有太多的经验。

I: Have you worked in a school?

A: No, I haven't.

面试者: 你在学校工作过吗?

求职者: 没有。

I: Do you have any sales experience?

A: Yes, I have stayed in this field for three years.

面试者: 你有销售经验吗?

求职者: 是的，我做这一行已经三年了。

I: Can you give me a general description of your former work?

A: I worked in a middle school, teaching English.

面试者: 能给我大体描述一下你以前的工作吗?

求职者: 我在一所中学做英语老师。

I: Have you ever been employed?

A: Yes, I worked in a fashion shop last summer as part-time salesgirl.

面试者: 你以前工作过吗?

求职者: 是的, 去年夏天我曾在一家时装店做兼职售货员。

I: Have you done any work in this field?

A: I am sorry to say that I have no experience in this field.

面试者: 你以前在这一领域干过吗?

求职者: 很抱歉, 我在这方面毫无经验。

I: Does your present employer know you are looking for another job?

A: No, I haven't discussed my career plans with my present employer, but I am sure he will understand.

面试者: 你现在的老板知道你在找另一份新的工作吗?

求职者: 不知道, 我没有和现在的老板谈论我的职业计划, 但我相信他会理解的。

情景单词快记忆

breakthrough 惊人的进展; 关键问题的解决	break the record 打破纪录
business background 工作经历	nominated 被提名的; 被任命的
operate 操作; 开动 (机器等); 经营 (厂矿)	organize 组织
originate 创始; 发明	overcome 克服 (困难等)
participate in 参加	business experience 工作经历
business history 工作经历	conduct 经营; 处理
control 控制	cost 成本; 费用
create 创造	decrease 减少
demonstrate 证明; 示范	accomplish 完成 (任务等)
achievement 工作成就; 业绩	adapt to 适应于
adept in 善于	administer 管理
advanced worker 先进工作者	analyze 分析
authorized 委任的; 核准的	be promoted to 被提升为
be proposed as 被提名为; 被推荐为	devise 设计; 发明
direct 指导	double 加倍; 翻一番

② 教育背景 Education Background

高频单句大放送

01. I graduate from Nanjing University.
我毕业于南京大学。

02. She got the MBA degree one years ago.
一年前她拿到了工商管理硕士学位。

03. I'm a M.A.
我是硕士。

04. Her brother is a PHD.
她的哥哥是位博士。

05. Which school are you studying in now?
你现在在哪所大学上学?

06. I'll try my best to get the B.A.
我将努力学习去获得学士学位。

07. What's your major?
你的专业是什么?

08. I'm specializing in English.
我的专业是英语。

09. I heard you're a junior college student.
我听说你是大专生。

10. His sister goes to a vocational school.
他的姐姐上职业专科学校。

口语问答面对面

(I = interviewer, A = applicant)

I: What is your major?
A: My major is Business Administration. I am especially interested in Marketing.
面试者: 你的专业是什么?
求职者: 我主修工商管理。我对市场营销很感兴趣。

I: What's your educational background?
A: Bachelor in English Literature.
面试者: 你的文凭是什么?
求职者: 英语语言文学学士学位。

I: What's your brother's highest degree?

A: PHD.

面试者: 你哥哥的最高学历是什么?

求职者: 博士。

I: Which school are you studying in now?

A: Beijing Language and Culture University.

面试者: 你现在在哪所大学上学?

求职者: 北京语言大学。

I: When will you graduate?

A: I'll graduate this summer.

面试者: 你什么时候毕业?

求职者: 我今年夏天毕业。

I: Which university are you attending?

A: I am attending Beijing Institute of Technology.

面试者: 你在哪所大学就读?

求职者: 我在北京理工大学就读。

I: Have you received any degrees?

A: Yes. First, I received my Bachelor degree in English Literature, and then a MBA degree.

面试者: 你有什么学历文凭吗?

求职者: 是的。首先,我在英语语言文学方面获得了学士学位,然后又获得了工商管理硕士学位。

I: What course do you like best?

A: Project Management. I was very interested in this course when I was a student. And I think it's very useful for my present work.

面试者: 你最喜欢什么课程?

求职者: 项目管理。上学时我对这一科目非常感兴趣。并且我认为这对我目前的工作很有用。

I: Where did you get your bachelor's degree?

A: Beijing Foreign Studies University.

面试者: 你在哪里读的本科?

求职者: 北京外国语大学。

I: How about your academic records at college?

A: I have been doing quite well at college.

面试者: 你大学的成绩如何?

求职者: 我在大学时学习很好。

I: Do you take any part-time jobs in your spare time?

A: Yes, I used to work as a tutor.

面试者: 学习之余, 你有没有做过兼职工作?

求职者: 是的, 我曾做过家教。

I: Do you feel that you have received a good general training?

A: Yes, I have studied in an English training program and a computer training program since I graduated from university. I am currently studying Finance at a training school.

面试者: 你认为你已经接受了很好的训练了吗?

求职者: 是的, 大学毕业后我接受过英语和电脑项目的培训。我现在在一所培训学校学习金融。

情景单词快记忆

education 学历	educational background 教育程度
educational history 学历	curriculum 课程
major 主修	minor 副修
educational highlights 课程重点部分	curriculum included 课程包括
specialized courses 专门课程	courses taken 所学课程
courses completed 所学课程	special training 特别训练
social practice 社会实践	part-time jobs 兼职
summer jobs 暑期工作	vacation jobs 假期工作
refresher course 进修课程	extracurricular activities 课外活动
physical activities 体育活动	recreational activities 娱乐活动
academic activities 学术活动	social activities 社会活动
rewards 奖励	scholarship 奖学金
"Three Goods" student 三好学生	excellent League member 优秀团员
excellent leader 优秀干部	student council 学生会

off-job training 脱产培训	in-job training 在职培训
educational system 学制	academic year 学年
semester 学期（美）	term 学期（英）
president 校长	vice-president 副校长

③ 语言能力 Languages Skills

🔵 高频单句大放送

01. How many languages can you speak?
    你能说几种语言？

02. Are you good at English?
    你擅长英语吗？

03. I have passed CET-6/4 (College English Test-6/4).
    我已经通过了大学英语六级 / 四级考试。

04. Last year, I passed BEC (Business English Certificate).
    去年，我通过了商务英语证书考试。

05. I majored in Japanese at university.
    我大学主修日语。

06. My foreign language at college is Russian.
    我在大学主修的外语是俄语。

07. I'll passed CELT (Comprehensive English Language Test).
    我将通过综合英语语言测试。

08. My score on TOEFL (Test of English as a Foreign Language) is 105.
    我的托福成绩是 105 分。

09. She got a high score on GRE (Graduate Record Examination).
    她在 GRE（研究生入学考试）中得了高分。

10. I studied English in the U. S. for three years.
    我在美国学了三年英语。

🔵 口语问答面对面

(I = interviewer, A = applicant)

I: Can you speak any foreign languages?

A: Yes, I can speak French, besides, I can also speak some Japanese. My major is French and minor in Japanese.

面试者: 你会说什么外语吗?

求职者: 是的，我会说法语，另外，我还会说些日语。我主修法语，辅修的是日语。

I: Can you speak any foreign languages?

A: I can speak English fluently.

面试者: 你会说什么外语吗?

求职者: 我能说一口流利的英语。

I: Really? Very good. How about Spanish?

A: Yes, I can speak Spanish very well, you know I'm interested in languages very much when I was at university. I also can speak a little Korean. But just a little. It's very fashion among young girls.

面试者: 是吗? 非常好。那么西班牙语呢?

求职者: 是的，我西班牙语说得很好，你知道我在大学里对语言非常感兴趣。我还会说一点韩语。但仅仅一点点。韩语在年轻女孩中非常流行。

I: Can you speak any foreign languages?

A: I can just speak a little Korean.

面试者: 你会说什么外语吗?

求职者: 我只会讲一点点的韩语。

I: Well, just one more question, would you like to be an interpreter?

A: Yes, I'd like to do it very well.

面试者: 那么，最后一个问题，你想做翻译吗?

求职者: 是的，我非常乐意。

I: How well can you speak Mandarin?

A: Very fluently.

面试者: 你的普通话说得如何?

求职者: 很流利。

I: Employees in our company must have a good command of English.

A: I can speak English fluently.

面试者: 我们公司的员工必须精通英语。

求职者: 我能熟练运用英语。

I: Can you manage English or Japanese conversations?

A: Yes, I'm sure I can.

面试者: 你能应付英语或日语的对话吗?

求职者: 是的，我能。

I: How about your spoken English?

A: My spoken English is fairly good enough to express myself fluently.

面试者: 你的英语口语如何?

求职者: 我可以用英语把自己的想法流利地表达出来。

I: How long have you learnt English?

A: More than ten years, I think.

面试者: 你学英语多久了?

求职者: 我想至少有十年了。

I: How well do you know English?

A: My English is very good. I can communicate with foreigners easily.

面试者: 你的英语程度如何?

求职者: 我的英语很好，我能轻松地和外国人交流。

I: Can you speak English?

A: Yes, I can speak English very well.

面试者: 你会说英语吗?

求职者: 是的，我讲得很好。

I: You're the just person we want to find.

A: Thank you. Next month I'll come here to work on time.

面试者: 你就是我们想要找的人。

求职者: 谢谢。下个月我会准时来这上班的。

情景单词快记忆

Afrikaans 南非语	Albanian 阿尔巴尼亚语
Amharic 阿姆哈拉语	Arabic 阿拉伯语
Armenian 亚美尼亚语	Azerbaijani 阿塞拜疆语
Bengali 孟加拉语	Bulgarian 保加利亚语
Burmese 缅甸语	Byelorussian 白俄罗斯语
Chinese 汉语	Czech 捷克语
Danish 丹麦语	Dutch 荷兰语

English 英语	Estonian 爱沙尼亚语
Finnish 芬兰语	Flemish 佛兰芒语
French 法语	Gaelic 盖尔语
Georgian 格鲁吉亚语	German 德语
Greek 希腊语	Gujarati 吉吉拉特语
Hebrew 希伯来语	Hindi 印地语
Hungarian 匈牙利语	Icelandic 冰岛语
Indonesian 印度尼西亚语	Italian 意大利语
Japanese 日语	Kazakh 哈萨克语
Kirgiz 吉尔吉斯语	Korean 朝鲜语
Lao 老挝语	Latvian 拉脱维亚语
Lithuanian 立陶宛语	Malagasy 马尔加什语
Malay 马来语	Maltese 马耳他语
Moldavian 摩尔达维亚语	Mongolian 蒙古语
Nepali 尼泊尔语	Norwegian 挪威语
Persian 波斯语	Polish 波兰语
Portuguese 葡萄牙语	Romanian 罗马尼亚语
Russian 俄语	Serbo-Croatian 塞尔维亚 - 克罗地亚语
Slovak 斯洛伐克语	Somali 索马里语
Spanish 西班牙语	Swedish 瑞典语
Tadzhik 塔吉克语	Thai 泰语
Turkmen 土库曼语	Turkish 土耳其语
Ukrainian 乌克兰语	Uzbek 乌兹别克语
Vietnamese 越南语	

读书笔记

15 职位应聘
Job Hunting

① 应聘教育人员 Applying for an Educator

🔵 高频单句大放送

01. What are your personality traits?
你的个性特征是什么？

02. Have you had any previous experience?
你以前有过相关经验吗？

03. I am a teaching assistant in an English training school.
我是一家英语培训学校的助教。

04. The interest is my main consideration in my job hunting.
选择工作时，我主要考虑兴趣。

05. I hope to learn some working skills and become a professional in this field.
我希望能获得工作技能，从而成为这个行业的专业人士。

06. I'd like to know if the company provides opportunities for further education.
我想了解贵公司是否提供继续学习的机会。

07. Here are my certificates of merit.
这是我的获奖证书。

08. I can start to work whenever it is convenient for you.
只要您方便，我随时都可以开始工作。

09. To tell you the truth, I'm an honest and reliable man.
说实话，我这个人诚实可靠。

10. I think it will be a good place for me to make use of my knowledge.
我认为这里是运用我知识的好地方。

🔵 口语问答面对面

Lily: Good morning, I am Lily. I came in answer to your advertisement for a teacher.

Tess: Good morning.

莉莉: 早上好，我是莉莉。我来应聘学校在广告上所招聘的老师一职。

苔丝: 早上好。

Tess: What teaching experience have you had?

Lily: I am afraid that I haven't had much teaching experience. I'm studying English Education in college. I want to get a job that would tie in with my studies.

苔丝: 你有哪些教学经验?

莉莉: 恐怕我没有什么教学经验。在大学时,我是学英语教育的。我希望找一份跟我的专业有关的工作。

Tess: What courses did you like most at university?

Lily: I like western culture and literature.

苔丝: 在大学,你最喜欢的课程是什么?

莉莉: 我最喜欢西方文化和文学。

Tess: How long would you like to work with us?

Lily: Two years at least.

苔丝: 你想在我们这里干多久?

莉莉: 最少两年。

Tess: Do you have any hobbies?

Lily: Yes, I like sports, reading and music.

苔丝: 你有什么爱好吗?

莉莉: 有,我喜欢运动、读书和听音乐。

Tess: Do you have any publications?

Lily: Yes. I have published some papers on the newspapers.

苔丝: 你有什么科研成果吗?

莉莉: 我有。我已经在报纸上发表过几篇文章。

Tess: We'll probably get back to you in a week.

Lily: Thanks a lot.

苔丝: 我们在一周之内可能会再和你联系。

莉莉: 非常感谢您。

Tess: Have you had any previous experience?

Lily: I am afraid that I haven't had much teaching experience.

苔丝: 你以前有过相关经验吗?

莉莉: 恐怕我没有什么教学经验。

Tess: Do you think you can make yourself understood in English?

Lily: Yes, I think I can in ordinary circumstances.

苔丝: 你认为你能用英语表达你的想法吗?

莉莉: 是的，一般情况下，我没有什么问题。

Tess: When can you start to work?

Lily: I can start to work whenever it is convenient for you.

苔丝: 你什么时候可以开始工作?

莉莉: 只要您方便，我随时都可以开始工作。

🔵 情景单词快记忆

primary/elementary school 小学	middle/high school 中学
university 大学	college 大专；大学
headmaster 小学校长	principal 中学校长
chancellor 大学名誉校长	vice president 大学副校长
president 大学校长	supervisor 论文导师
acting president 大学代理校长	preschool education 学前教育
special education 特殊教育	compulsory education 义务教育
higher education/tertiary education 高等教育	quality-oriented education 素质教育
junior high school 初中	senior high school 高中
cultivate one's taste and temperament 陶冶情操	to combine ability with character/equal stress on integrity and ability 德才兼备

② 应聘金融财会人员 Applying for a Financial Accounting Staff

🔵 高频单句大放送

01. Have you brought your certificates?
    你的学历证明带来了吗?

02. Do you have any particular conditions that you would like our firm to take into consideration?
    你有什么让我们公司考虑的特殊情况吗?

03. My past experience is closely related to this job.
    我过去的经验与这份工作有密切的联系。

04. Do you have any experience in banking?
   你在银行业方面有经验吗？

05. During my studies at the university, accounting was my special field of interests.
   大学期间，会计是我特别感兴趣的科目。

06. I have a good all-round knowledge of accountant.
   我对会计工作有全面的了解。

07. At the college I served as financial secretary of the Students Union.
   大学期间，我曾出任学生会财务秘书一职。

08. I have been employed as a junior accountant in an import and export company for two years.
   我在一家进出口公司担任了两年初级会计员。

09. I shall bring to the job the willingness to work and an eagerness to improve.
   我在工作中乐于学习、渴望提高。

10. I have a comparatively good understanding for this position.
   对这一职位，我有较好的理解。

🔵 口语问答面对面

Louise: Please sit down. Is your major accounting?

Frank: Yes. I am engaged in accounting for one year.

路易斯: 请坐。你的专业是会计学吗？

弗兰克: 是的。我从事会计这一行业已经一年了。

Louise: What are your responsibilities at your present work?

Frank: My work includes various routine bookkeeping and basic accounting tasks.

路易斯: 你现在的工作主要负责什么？

弗兰克: 我的工作主要包括各种常规性记账和基本的会计工作。

Louise: Are you familiar with the financial and tax regulations?

Frank: I think so.

路易斯: 你熟悉金融税务制度吗？

弗兰克: 我觉得自己还可以。

Louise: Have you had any previous experience?

Frank: I have been employed as a junior accountant in an import and export company for two years.

路易斯: 你有相关的经验吗?
弗兰克: 我在一家进出口公司担任了两年初级会计员。

Louise: Have you brought your certificates?
Frank: Yes, here you are.
路易斯: 你的学历证明带来了吗?
弗兰克: 是的, 给你。

Louise: Do you have any particular conditions that you would like our firm to take into consideration?
Frank: May I ask for an apartment?
路易斯: 你有什么让我们公司考虑的特殊情况吗?
弗兰克: 我可以要一套公寓房吗?

Louise: Do you have any experience in banking?
Frank: Yes, I have worked two years in this field.
路易斯: 你在银行业方面有经验吗?
弗兰克: 是的, 我已经在这行做了两年了。

Louise: How would your friends or colleagues describe you?
Frank: They would say Frank is an honest, hard-working and responsible man.
路易斯: 你的朋友或同事怎样形容你?
弗兰克: 他们会说弗兰克讲诚信, 工作很努力, 责任心很强。

Louise: Why did you leave your last job?
Frank: Well, I am hoping to get a better position.
路易斯: 你为什么离职呢?
弗兰克: 我希望能获得一份更好的工作。

Louise: Very good. You are the very person we want.
Frank: Thank you very much.
路易斯: 很好。你正是我们想要的人。
弗兰克: 非常感谢。

情景单词快记忆

venture capital 风险资本	virtual value 虚拟价值
patent & trademark office 专利与商标局	book value 账面价值

physical capital 实际资本	collective market cap 市场资本总值
consolidation 兼并	transparency 透明度
damage-control machinery 安全顾问	intellectual property 知识产权
bribery 行贿	cook the book 做假账
accounting firm 会计事务所	pension fund 养老基金
mutual fund 共同基金	traded company/trading enterprise 上市公司
depreciation 贬值	deficit 赤字
bad debt 坏账	macroeconomic 宏观经济

③ 应聘销售人员 Applying for a Salesman

高频单句大放送

01. Do you like your present job?
你喜欢现在这个工作吗？

02. I'd like to hear your opinion.
我想听听你的意见。

03. Do you have any experience in sales promotion?
你有做促销的经验吗？

04. Are you familiar with our pay scale?
你熟悉我们的薪金情况吗？

05. How do you usually handle criticism?
你通常如何处理别人的批评？

06. What is your strongest trait?
你个性上最大的特点是什么？

07. The vocational training I have received fits me very well for this job.
我接受的职业培训使我非常适合这个工作。

08. I am cheerful and willing to communicate with others.
我的个性开朗，愿意与人沟通。

09. I will try to present my ideas in order to get my points across.
我会提出我的看法，使对方了解我的观点。

10. Of course, I am afraid I'm not the possible candidate.
当然，我不一定是合适人选。

口语问答面对面

Ms. May: To start with, tell me something about your education, please.

Desmond: All right. I graduated from a trade university. I major in marketing.

梅女士: 首先，请谈谈你的教育状况。

德斯蒙德: 好。我毕业于一所贸易大学，所学专业是市场营销。

Ms. May: We need a salesman and the work entails much travel. How do you think of it?

Desmond: In my opinion, I'd rather secure my careers before I settle down in a family. If the work needs me to travel, I will do.

梅女士: 我们需要一名销售人员，而且这份工作要求经常出差。你怎么看待这个问题?

德斯蒙德: 在我看来，我宁可先干一番事业，而不愿意过早成家安定下来。如果工作需要出差的话，我会这么做的。

Ms. May: Why are you interested in our company?

Desmond: I think working in this company would provide me with a good opportunity to use my knowledge.

梅女士: 你为什么对我们公司感兴趣?

德斯蒙德: 我认为贵公司会为我提供很好的机会以运用我的知识。

Ms. May: What is your strongest trait?

Desmond: I am cheerful and willing to communicate with others.

梅女士: 你个性上最大的特点是什么?

德斯蒙德: 我的个性开朗，愿意与人沟通。

Ms. May: How do you usually handle criticism?

Desmond: I will try to present my ideas in order to get my points across.

梅女士: 你通常如何处理别人的批评?

德斯蒙德: 我会提出我的看法，使对方了解我的观点。

Ms. May: Why do you consider yourself qualified for this job?

Desmond: The vocational training I have received fits me very well for this job.

梅女士: 你为什么觉得自己适合这份工作?

德斯蒙德: 我接受的职业培训使我非常适合这个工作。

Ms. May: By the way, would you describe yourself as extroverted or more introverted?

Desmond: I think I am quite outgoing. I like cooperating with others and getting the job done by working together.

梅女士: 顺便问问，你认为自己性格是更外向还是更内向？

德斯蒙德: 我认为自己是外向的。我喜欢跟人合作，和大家一起完成任务。

Ms. May: Do you have any experience in sales?

Desmond: I worked as a salesperson as a part-time job.

梅女士: 你有销售的经验吗？

德斯蒙德: 我做过兼职的销售人员。

Ms. May: Do you have any questions about the job?

Desmond: No, I don't. I will do my best if this company employs me.

梅女士: 关于工作，你还有什么问题吗？

德斯蒙德: 没有了。如果公司聘用我，我会尽最大努力工作的。

Desmond: Thank you.

Ms. May: We will call you as soon as we decide it.

德斯蒙德: 谢谢。

梅女士: 我们决定后会尽快电话通知你的。

情景单词快记忆

break the record 打破纪录	business background 工作经历
business experience 工作经历	business history 工作经历
conduct 经营；处理	control 控制
cost 成本；费用	create 创造
decrease 减少	demonstrate 证明；示范
design 设计	develop 开发；发挥
devise 设计；发明	direct 指导
double 加倍；翻一番	duties 职责
earn 获得；赚取	effect 效果；作用

16 工作与学习 Work and Study

① 谈论工作 Talking About the Vocation

🔵 高频单句大放送

01. What kind of job do you want?
   你想要什么样的工作?

02. She's deciding on her career.
   她正在考虑做什么工作。

03. I'm working for a foreign trade company.
   我在一家外贸公司工作。

04. I want to be an interpreter.
   我想当一名翻译。

05. I think teacher doesn't suit me, because I have no patience at all.
   我认为当老师不适合我，因为我一点耐心都没有。

06. I have to give up the ideal of becoming a hostess.
   我不得不放弃当一位主持人的理想。

07. I have worked as a lawyer for ten years, and I like my vocation very much.
   我已经干律师这行十年了，我非常喜欢这份职业。

08. I want to change my job.
   我想换个职业。

09. All the vocations are equal.
   所有的职业都是平等的。

10. What do you do for a living?
   你是干哪一行的?

🔵 口语问答面对面

Jasmine: Hello, James. I haven't seen you for ages. How are you getting along these days?
James: I'm well, Jasmine.
茉莉: 嗨，詹姆斯。好久不见。最近怎么样啊?

詹姆斯: 我很好，茉莉。

James: How about you?

Jasmine: Not bad, considering I'm going to be fifty next June.

詹姆斯: 你呢?

茉莉: 不错，考虑到下个六月我就要 50 岁了。

Jasmine: I heard you've got a new job. What do you do now?

James: I'm working in the fabrics division of a large chemical company.

茉莉: 我听说你找到了新工作，你现在做什么?

詹姆斯: 我在一家大的化工公司纤维部工作。

Jasmine: What do you do for a living?

James: I'm working for a foreign trade company.

茉莉: 你是干哪一行的?

詹姆斯: 我在一家外贸公司工作。

Jasmine: What kind of job do you want ?

James: I want to be an interpreter.

茉莉: 你想要什么样的工作?

詹姆斯: 我想当一名翻译。

Jasmine: What kind of job do you want?

James: I think editor is the just job I have been seeking all the time.

茉莉: 你想要什么样的工作?

詹姆斯: 我认为编辑就是我一直想要找的工作。

Jasmine: Sounds interesting.

James: Yes, it's really a very exciting job. At that moment we are developing a new fibre.

茉莉: 听起来很有趣。

詹姆斯: 是的，确实很有趣。工作时我们要合成新的纤维。

Jasmine: Really? Well you've always been clever. I knew you'd do something very interesting. Do you have to travel around?

James: Not really, I work in the lab most of the time. But I sometimes go to the US.

茉莉: 是吗? 你总是那么的聪明。我知道你们将做些很有趣的事情。你们要到处出差吗?

詹姆斯: 事实上不是的，我大部分时间在实验室里工作。但有时会去美国。

Jasmine: How long have you been doing this job?
James: About two years.
茉莉: 这个工作你做了多长时间?
詹姆斯: 大约两年了。

Jasmine: Well, James, you must come and see me sometime and tell me all about it over a cup of tea.
James: I certainly will.
茉莉: 那么詹姆斯，你有时间一定要来看我，喝茶时和我说说关于你的工作上的一切。
詹姆斯: 当然会。

情景单词快记忆

improve 改进；提高	increase 增加
influence 影响	initiate 创始；开创
innovate 改革；革新	inspired 受启发的；受鼓舞的
install 安装	integrate 使结合；使一体化
introduce 采用；引进	invent 发明
invest 投资	job title 职位
justified 经证明的；合法化的	launch 开办（新企业）
lead 领导	lengthen 延长
lessen 减少（生产成本）	level 水平
localize 使地方化	mastered 精通的
modernize 使现代化	motivate 促进；激发
negotiate 谈判	nominated 被提名的；被任命的
occupational history 工作经历	operate 操作；开动（机器等）；经营（厂矿）
organize 组织	originate 创始；发明
overcome 克服（困难等）	participate in 参加
perfect 使完善；改善	perform 执行；履行
plan 计划	position 职位

② 学习与工作 Study and Work

01. What courses are you planning to take?
你打算修些什么课程?

02. Are you busy with your study this term?
你这学期学习忙吗?

03. I'm very good at Chinese.
我语文学得很好。

04. I'm very poor in Math.
我的数学很差。

05. Nowadays more and more people are out of jobs.
现在失业的人越来越多。

06. He landed with another job soon after he left his former company.
他离开了以前的公司后很快找到了另一份工作。

07. Have you done anything like that before?
你以前有没有做过类似的工作?

08. The work is very boring.
这工作真无聊。

09. I want to work in the banking industry.
我想在银行工作。

10. That's a job that pays well.
那份工作收入不错。

Paul: You're graduating this year, right?
Amy: Yes, in July.
保罗: 你今年毕业, 是吗?
艾米: 是的, 7月毕业。

Paul: Have you tried looking for a job?
Amy: No, I am planning to do some further studies.
保罗: 你有没有试着找工作?
艾米: 没有, 我打算进一步深造。

Paul: Do you like your present job?

Amy: The work is very boring.
保罗: 你喜欢你现在的工作吗?
艾米: 这工作真无聊。

Paul: What other subjects did you learn?
Amy: Business administration.
保罗: 你还学过什么其他的课程?
艾米: 工商管理。

Paul: What are you going to study?
Amy: I want to study economics.
保罗: 你打算学什么?
艾米: 我想学习经济学。

Paul: I hear you are going to Britain.
Amy: Yes.
保罗: 我听说你要去英国。
艾米: 是的。

Paul: Have you applied to any universities?
Amy: I'd like to be a postgraduate in accounting at Cambridge University.
保罗: 你是否向一些大学提出申请了呢?
艾米: 我想申请剑桥大学会计学的硕士生。

Paul: You'd better apply as soon as possible. There are many excellent students applying for this university.
Amy: Yes. I've just finished my application letter.
保罗: 你最好尽快申请。有很多优秀的学生都在申请这所大学。
艾米: 是的, 我刚写完申请信。

Amy: Could you go over it for me?
Paul: Let me see the letter. No, we don't write letters in this way. Your letter should be clear, concise, courteous and correct.
艾米: 你能帮我看看吗?
保罗: 让我看看。不行, 我们不这样写信。你的信应该清楚、简洁、有礼貌, 而且还要正确。

Amy: I only need to tell what I want and what I require. No unnecessary words.
Paul: Yes. Hope you can get the green light.

艾米: 我只需要写清楚我要做什么就行了。不用写多余的话。

保罗: 对。希望你能获得批准。

情景单词快记忆

specialized course 专业课	school timetable 课程表
extracurricular activities 课外活动	instruction after class 课外辅导
class discussion 课堂讨论	seminar 大学的研究小组；讨论会
teaching program/syllabus 教学大纲	content of courses 教学内容
commencement 毕业典礼	graduation appraisal 毕业鉴定
graduation field work 毕业实习	diploma/graduation certificate 毕业证书
online teaching/education 网上教学	correspondence course 函授课程
professional personnel 专业人才	talent exchange 人才交流
brain drain 人才流失	people of vision 有识之士
brain trust/think tank 智囊团	

③ 安排老板日程 Making Schedule for the Boss

高频单句大放送

01. Would you please file these documents for me?
你可以帮我把这些文件归下类吗？

02. I've arranged today's reports for you to examine.
我已将今天的报告整理好了，请你过目。

03. Here are all the documents and information you required.
这是你需要的所有文件和资料。

04. I'll list down all the documents.
我会整理这些文件的。

05. I am at your disposal, Mr. Manager.
经理先生，我听候你的吩咐。

06. Have you found those files I requested?
我要的那些档案资料都找到了吗？

07. But you are going to have to re-do this planning.
我想你应该重写一遍这个计划。

08. What's my schedule for today, Jasmine?
我今天的安排是什么，茉莉？

09. I'll get those plans over to your office by next Monday.
我会在下周一前把计划送到你办公室。

10. Do you have any particular instructions for this?
对于这个还有其他什么特别的要求吗？

口语问答面对面

Secretary: Sir, Mr. James from editing would like your opinion on this report.
Boss: I'm too busy right now. Would you please put it in my in-box? I'll add it to my PIM's To-Do list.
秘书: 先生，编辑部的詹姆斯先生想请您看一下他的报告。
老板: 我现在太忙了。请把它放在我的信箱里。我会把它加在我的商务通执行表中。

Secretary: Sally Jones from photography wants to discuss the Easter campaign.
Boss: Hmm, yes, that's a key issue we still have to resolve.
秘书: 摄影部的萨利·琼斯想和您讨论复活节的活动。
老板: 嗯，好，那是一个要解决的关键问题。

Boss: What's my schedule like?
Secretary: The earliest slot available is in two days.
老板: 我的日程安排是什么？
秘书: 最近一项安排在两天后。

Boss: OK, make an appointment for a meeting with her. While you're at it, make an appointment with the client after the meeting with Sally. We'll discuss the final design and the contract.
Secretary: According to your plan, you wanted to check on the Farley project today.
老板: 好，跟她安排一次会面。同时安排一下随后与客户的会面。我们要谈一下最终设计和合同的问题。
秘书: 根据您的日程表，您今天要检查一下法利项目。

Boss: No need. The design's available. Now, where did I put the memos for last week's meetings? Oh, there they are! Let me see the agenda for this meeting, please.
Secretary: Right here, sir.

老板: 不需要了。设计已经有了。我把上周的会议记录放在哪了? 哦, 在那儿! 请让我看一下这次开会的议程。

秘书: 给您, 先生。

Secretary: Do you have any particular instructions for this?

Boss: Nothing.

秘书: 对于这个还有其他什么特别的要求吗?

老板: 没有了。

Boss: Have you found those files I requested?

Secretary: Yes, they're here.

老板: 我要的那些档案资料都找到了吗?

秘书: 是的, 在这儿呢。

Secretary: Would you please file these documents for me?

Boss: Of course, I will.

秘书: 你可以帮我把这些文件归下类吗?

老板: 当然了。

Secretary: Here are all the documents and information you required.

Boss: Put them on my desk.

秘书: 这是你要的文件和资料。

老板: 放在我桌上。

情景单词快记忆

intercom 内部通话系统	document 公文
cabinet 文件柜	locker 锁柜
personal computer 个人电脑	copier 复印机
drawer 抽屉	tray 文件盒
paper shredder 碎纸机	typewriter 打字机
book 账本	clip 弹簧夹子
cigarette 香烟	ashtray 烟灰缸
punch 打孔机	sponge 海绵
adhesive notes 可粘便笺	memo pad 备忘录
name card 名片	file 档案

17 工作详情 Job Details

① 接案 Receiving Cases

高频单句大放送

01. A lawyer shall not represent both parties involved in the same case.
律师不得在同一案件中为双方当事人担任代理。

02. A lawyer should assist in maintaining the integrity and competence of the legal profession.
律师应该帮助维护律师界的正直和业务能力。

03. A lawyer should assist the legal profession in fulfilling its duty to make legal counsel available.
律师应帮助律师界履行其提供法律顾问的义务。

04. A lawyer should preserve the confidences and secrets of client.
律师应当为当事人保密。

05. A lawyer should represent a client competently.
律师应当称职地担任当事人的代理。

06. Can you contact the solicitors representing the vendors?
你能与代表卖方的律师联系吗?

07. Counsel is instructed to settle the defense.
律师接受指示处理辩护事项。

08. Counsel for the plaintiff opposed the defendant's application for an adjournment.
原告律师反对被告的休庭申请。

09. Counsel must not lead the witness.
律师不得诱导证人。

10. Counsel prevailed upon the judge to grant an adjournment.
律师劝说法官休庭。

口语问答面对面

Mike: Hello, I'm here for a consultation regarding civil law.

Lawyer: Yes, please.

麦克: 您好，我想咨询一下民法方面的问题。

律师: 请讲。

Mike: My neighbors are causing me to lose sleep. They are always singing and dancing late into the night.

Lawyer: Oh, I see. For a case like this, we'll arrange for a lawyer to go visiting your neighbor with you.

麦克: 我邻居让我根本睡不着觉。他们总是唱歌跳舞到大半夜。

律师: 哦，明白了。对于这种案子，我们通常会安排个律师去跟您的邻居交涉。

Mike: I spoke to them several times before. I don't think having a lawyer present is going to help.

Lawyer: In that case, we'll contact the police. If they find enough evidence, they'll force your neighbors to comply.

麦克: 我和他们都谈过好几次了。我看律师去谈也不会管用的。

律师: 这样的话，我们就只能通知警方了，如果证据确凿，警方就能强令他们夜间安静些。

Policeman: What can I do for you ?

Student: I'm John Smith. I am here to report a stole bike.

警察: 有什么需要帮忙的吗?

学生: 我叫约翰·史密斯，我的自行车丢了，来报案。

Policeman: OK, when did you find out your bike was stolen?

Student: Just about ten minutes ago, at around 5:30.

警察: 什么时候被偷的?

学生: 就十分钟前，五点半左右。

Policeman: And where did you leave your bike?

Student: At the left corner of the cafeteria, just near the law faculty building.

警察: 你把车放哪了?

学生: 放在食堂的左侧了，就是挨着法学院教师楼的那侧。

Policeman: What kind of bike do you have?

Student: It is a mountain bike, three years old, red.

警察: 你的车是什么样子的?

学生: 是一辆红色山地车，用了三年了。

Student: What are the chances of finding it?

Policeman: Not too large I'm afraid. There are about ten thousand bikes on campus. It's like trying to find a needle in a haystack.

学生: 找回来的可能性有多大?

警察: 恐怕不大。学校里有一万辆自行车。这就像大海捞针一样。

情景单词快记忆

court acceptance fee 案件受理费	case 案子
monopolize lawsuits 包揽诉讼	appellee 被上诉人
respondent 被告人	defense pleadings 辩护词
defense lawyer 辩护律师	point of defense 辩护要点
submission 辩护意见	award 裁决书
established evidence 采信的证据	conveyancing 产权转让
exhibit 出示的证据	appear in court 出庭
summons 传票	representation 代理词
statement of the parties 当事人陈述	investigation record 调查笔录
legal consultant 法律顾问	senior partner 高级合伙人
senior lawyer 高级律师	lawyer license 律师执业证
civil case 民事案件	

② 办案 Handling a Case

高频单句大放送

01. After ten hours' questioning by the police, the accused man confessed.
    经过警方十个小时的审问, 被告供认了犯罪事实。

02. At this point the police interfered.
    此时警方介入进来。

03. He is wanted by the police.
    他被警方通缉。

04. The chief constable applied for an order of mandamus directing the justices to rehear the case.
    警察局申请获得履行职务令, 以命令法官重新审理该案。

05. The confession was extracted under torture by the police.
供认是警方严刑逼供得到的。

06. The police are close to solving the crime.
警方即将破案。

07. The police were accused of tampering with the evidence.
警察被指控篡改证词。

08. The post mortem was carried out or was conducted by the police pathologist.
由警察病理学家进行验尸。

09. The thief surrendered himself to the police.
小偷向警方自首。

10. When he offered to give information to the police, he was granted immunity from prosecution.
当他主动给警察提供信息时，他被免予起诉。

🔵 口语问答面对面

Policeman: What's your name?
Suspect: My name is James.
警察: 你叫什么名字?
嫌疑犯: 我叫詹姆斯。

Policeman: What's your nationality?
Suspect: American.
警察: 你是什么国籍?
嫌疑犯: 美国。

Policeman: What's your relationship with the victim?
Suspect: I don't know him.
警察: 你跟受害者是什么关系?
嫌疑犯: 我不认识他。

Policeman: Why did you attack the victim?
Suspect: He beat me first when I tried to stop him from grabbing my bag and running away.
警察: 你为什么攻击受害者?
嫌疑犯: 我试图阻止他夺走我的包逃跑时，他先打我的。

Policeman: Were you in the house when the burglary occurred?

Victim: Yes, I was in.
警察: 盗窃案发生时，你在家吗？
受害者: 是的，我在家。

Policeman: Do you know the person who attacked you?
Victim: No, I don't know him.
警察: 你认识袭击你的人吗？
受害者: 不认识。

Policeman: Did you threaten the victim with your weapon?
Victim: No.
警察: 你是否用武器威胁过受害者？
受害者: 没有。

情景单词快记忆

investigate 调查；研究	needle 针；指针；刺激；针状物
haystack 干草堆	confess 承认；坦白；忏悔；供认
interfere 干涉；妨碍；打扰	mandamus 命令书；书面训练
justice 司法；法律制裁；正义；法官；审判员	torture 折磨；歪曲；拷问
tamper 篡改；干预；损害；削弱	pathologist 病理学家
surrendered himself to 投降；屈服	immunity 免疫力；豁免权；免除
prosecution 起诉；检举；进行；经营	Constable 警员
Senior Constable 高级警员	Sergeant 警长
Station Sergeant 警署警长	Probationary Inspector of Police 见习督察
Inspector of Police 督察	Senior Inspector of Police 高级督察
Chief Inspector of Police 总督察	Superintendent of Police 警司
Senior Superintendent of Police 高级警司	Chief Superintendent of Police 总警司

③ 护理病人 Nursing the Sick

高频单句大放送

01. He works in a hospital.
    他在医院工作。

02. Both my parents are doctors.
我的父母都是医生。

03. He isn't a doctor, is he?
他不是医生，对吗?

04. The doctor is often more to be feared than the disease.
医生往往比疾病更令人生畏。

05. A good surgeon must have an eagle's eye, a lion's heart and a lady's hand.
出色的外科医生必须眼明胆大和有一双灵巧的手。

06. The gown a surgeon wears during an operation is usually green.
外科医生在做手术时穿的手术服通常是绿色的。

07. It was assumed doctor was the profession with the promise of the greatest financial reward.
据说，医生这一职业反映了当时最好的职业待遇水平。

08. The doctor was barred from practising after he was proved guilty of improper behaviour.
在被证明有不当行为后，这个医生被禁止行医。

09. The prescription of drugs is a doctor's responsibility.
开药方是医生的职责。

10. An alert pharmacist will save a doctor from his mistake by querying a prescription.
警惕性很高的药剂师应对处方提出疑问而避免医生的错误。

口语问答面对面

N: Hello! How are you feeling now?
C: I am still having a headache.
护士: 你好，现在感觉怎么样?
病人: 我仍然感到头疼。

C: When are my relatives allowed to visit me ?
N: The visit time is from four to six in the afternoon. My name is Jone, head nurse of the ward. Doctor Smith is director of the ward, but Doctor Bush is responsible for your treatment. He is kind and considerate. So you are in good hands.
病人: 什么时候我家里人可以来看我?
护士: 探视时间是下午 4~6 点钟。我叫琼，是这个病区的护士长，病区主任是史密斯先生，布什医生负责你的治疗。他人很好而且细心周到。你在这儿会得到很好的照顾。

C: How about meals?

N: Meal times are 7 a.m. for breakfast, 12 noon for lunch, and 6 p.m. for dinner, we serve a variety of Chinese, Muslim and western food. Our clinical dietician is available for advice on special diets. The doctor has ordered a soft diet for you these days. We will put you on the regular diet when your condition has improved.

病人：这里的膳食情况怎么样？

护士：医院早餐时间是 7 点，午饭是 12 点，晚饭是 6 点开始，供应品种繁多的中餐、清真食物和西餐。我们的临床营养师可对特殊的饭菜进行调配。根据医嘱你这几天要进软食，当病情改善后可调整为正常饮食。

C: That's fine. When will the doctor come to see me?

N: The ward rounds and treatment start at 8 a.m. every morning.

病人：好的，医生什么时候来看我？

护士：每天上午 8 点是医生查房和治疗时间。

N: When do you expect to be back to work?

C: They said not until next week, but I might sneak out a little early for a half day.

护士：您估计什么时候能回去工作？

病人：他们说至少得下周，不过我可能会提早溜回去。

N: I hope it's nothing serious.

C: It's nothing. I'll be back up and around by the end of this week.

护士：我希望问题不太严重。

病人：没什么。我这个周末就可以活蹦乱跳地回去了。

N: So, how are you feeling?

C: Better than I thought. They might even release me a day earlier.

护士：你感觉如何了？

病人：比我想象的要好得多。他们可能会让我提前一天出院。

N: You're tough. You'll be back on your feet in no time.

C: Yeah, that's what I thought, but this thing has really kicked my ass.

护士：你很坚强。你很快就能重新站起来了。

病人：是啊，我也是这么想的。不过这件事情真是给了我不小的教训。

C: Thank you very much for your information and advice. How can I reach you if I need you?

N: The panel at the head of the bed is equipped with a nurse-call system. To alert the staff at the nurse's station, press the button by the bedside. A nurse will attend to your needs as soon as possible. Please press this button any time you need me, someone will always come if I am not there.

病人: 谢谢你给我提供的信息和建议，如果我还想找你的话怎样才能联系到你？

护士: 在你的床头有个呼叫开关，连接护士呼叫系统。按下这个开关可以提醒护士站的工作人员，护士会立即过来帮助你。你需要我的帮助可以随时按这个开关，如果我不在那里会有其他护士来帮你。

C: Thank you. You have made me feel much better.

N: You are welcome. In case of any questions, please ask any of the staff here. We'll be glad to offer you our help.

病人: 谢谢你的介绍，我现在感觉好多了。

护士: 不客气。如果有什么问题，你可以随时询问我们在这里的工作人员，我们很高兴能为你提供帮助。

情景单词快记忆

director of the hospital 院长

physician in charge 主治医生

resident physician 住院医生

intern/interne 实习医生

head nurse 护士长

anaesthetist 麻醉师

internist/physician 内科医生

surgeon 外科医生

brain specialist 脑科专家

dentist 牙科医生

dermatologist 皮肤科医生

gynecologist 妇科医生

heart specialist 心脏病专家

obstetrician 产科医生

paediatrician 小儿科医生

plastic surgeon 整形外科医生

out-patient 门诊病人

in-patient 住院病人

medical patient 内科病人

surgical patient 外科病人

obstetrical patient 产科病人

emergency case 急诊病人

18 工作情绪 Job Emotion

① 喜欢工作 Enjoying My Work

高频单句大放送

01. I really enjoy my work.
我非常喜欢我的工作。

02. Did you find a good job?
你找到一份不错的工作了吗？

03. Work can be hard, but it's good if you enjoy it.
工作有时很辛苦，但是你喜欢自己的工作这很好。

04. You work so hard! Nearly every day of the week!
你工作非常辛苦！几乎每天都工作！

05. I guess most people don't really love their work —it's just a job.
我想大多数人并不真正喜欢他们的工作——只是工作。

06. It's long hours but I like my work.
工作时间长，但是我喜欢我的工作。

07. I am satisfied with my job.
我对这份工作很满意。

08. This job is suitable for me.
这份工作很适合我。

09. I have a well-paid job.
我的收入不错。

10. The career offers a challenge.
这份职业很有挑战性。

口语问答面对面

Falcon: What do you think of your job?

Jasmine: To tell the truth, the work is very hard and boring, but I like it and it suits me very well.

福尔肯: 你觉得你的工作怎么样？

贾思敏: 说实话，我的工作有点难而且还很枯燥，但是我很喜欢它，觉得那很适合我。

Falcon: So, what do you do ?
Jasmine: I work in a publishing house.
福尔肯: 那么，你是干什么的?
贾思敏: 我在出版社工作。

Jasmine: How about you?
Falcon: Mine is not hard. And I think it's interesting.
贾思敏: 你呢?
福尔肯: 我的工作不难。我认为很有趣。

Jasmine: What do you do then?
Falcon: I'm a clerk in a mall.
贾思敏: 那么你是干什么的呢?
福尔肯: 我在商场工作。

Jasmine: How do you like your job here?
Falcon: It's interesting. I like being an editor.
贾思敏: 你觉得你在这儿的工作怎样?
福尔肯: 挺有意思的。我喜欢做编辑。

Jasmine: Why?
Falcon: I like talking to writers. I get to meet lots of interesting people.
贾思敏: 为什么?
福尔肯: 我喜欢和作者交流。可以有机会碰到很多有趣的人。

Jasmine: Do you have any complaints?
Falcon: No, I have no complaints.
贾思敏: 你有什么不满吗?
福尔肯: 没有，我没有什么不满。

Jasmine: I hear there are many opportunities to move up in this company. Is that true?
Falcon: Yes. You'll have many opportunities to grow in this company as long as you do well.
贾思敏: 我听说在这个公司有很多升职的机会。这是真的吗?
福尔肯: 是真的。只要你干得好，在这个公司就会有很多发展机会。

Jasmine: How do you like your job here?
Falcon: This job pays well.
贾思敏: 你觉得你在这儿的工作怎么样？
福尔肯: 这个工作的报酬不错。

Jasmine: How do you like your job here?
Falcon: It's hard but very challenging.
贾思敏: 你觉得在这儿的工作怎么样？
福尔肯: 工作虽然辛苦，但很有挑战性。

🌐 情景单词快记忆

Ministry of Labour 劳工部	occupational disease 职业病
labour market 劳工市场；劳务市场	stenographer 速记员
full employment 全日制工作	telephone operator 电话接线员
seasonal work 季节工作	programmer 电脑程序员
piecework 计件工作	shorthand typist 速记打字员
timework 计时工作	public servants 公务员
teamwork 联合工作	national public servant 国家公务员
shift work 换班工作	local public service employee 地方公务员
vacancy 空缺；空额	nation railroad man 国有铁路职员
work permit 工作许可证	

② 不喜欢工作 Disliking My Job

🌐 高频单句大放送

01. I'm quite dissatified with this job.
我对这份工作很不满意。

02. I'm tired with this boring job.
我厌倦了这种无聊的工作。

03. The work really turns me off.
这份工作使我很反感。

04. The salary is very low.
工资太低了。

05. I've never liked working in this company.
我从没喜欢在这家公司上班。

06. I'm under great pressure now.
我现在的压力很大。

07. I feel like wiped out.
我感觉累垮掉了。

08. I'm really depressed in this company.
在这家公司我感觉很郁闷。

09. I don't have any zest for work.
我毫无工作热情。

10. I can't bear doing the same thing day by day.
我无法忍受日复一日做同样的工作。

口语问答面对面

Jasmine: You look really wiped out.
Bessie: I had meetings back-to-back all morning. Then the printer broke in the middle of putting together the Wix Soap presentation, and the phone rang off the hook from the minute I walked into the office.
茉莉: 你好像全垮了。
贝西: 今天上午是连轴开会。在准备 Wix 香皂介绍时打印机又出了问题。电话从我一进门就响个不停。

Jasmine: May I put in for a transfer?
Manager: Yes, I'd be delighted if you did.
茉莉: 我可以申请调动吗?
经理: 可以，你要这样做了，我会很高兴的。

Jasmine: Do you mind if I speak frankly?
Manager: Not at all. Go ahead.
茉莉: 我实话实说您介意吗?
经理: 一点也不介意。你说吧。

Jasmine: Is it all right for me to come in now?
Manager: Well, I'm pretty busy, but…all right, come in.
茉莉: 我现在可以进来吗?
经理: 我很忙，不过……好吧，进来吧。

Jasmine: What can I do for you?

Manager: Do you mind if I sit down?

茉莉: 有事儿吗?

经理: 您介意我坐下来吗?

Manager: Take a seat. Now, what can I do for you?

Jasmine: I want to leave the department.

经理: 坐吧。现在说吧,什么事?

茉莉: 我想离开这个部门。

Jasmine: Do you think I could put in for a transfer?

Manager: Yes, but why should you want to do that?

茉莉: 您认为我能申请调动吗?

经理: 可以,不过你为什么那样做呢?

Jasmine: Not a good day, I hate to tell you that Mr. Emory wants to see the designs for the Ad tomorrow morning.

Bessie: I can't believe it! I guess I'll be here until ten again tonight! I just feel uncomfortable these days.I'm really tired. If I have another chance, I'll quit this job quickly.

茉莉: 真不是个好日子。我真不好意思告诉你,埃莫里先生明天上午想要看广告设计。

贝西: 真难以置信! 我想今天晚上又得在这熬到十点了。我最近觉得很不舒服。我真的很累了,如果有其他的机会,我会立刻放弃这个工作的。

Jasmine: So you don't like your present job, do you?

Bessie: To be frank, it always has many trivial things to do. You know it's very boring.

茉莉: 所以说你是不喜欢这份工作了,是吗?

贝西: 说实话,总是有那么多琐碎的事情要去做。非常烦人。

Jasmine: Why don't you try to find another job which you like?

Bessie: Actually I have sent many resumes, but still have no response. But for earning money to support my family, I'll resign at once.

茉莉: 为什么你不去找找别的你喜欢的工作呢?

贝西: 事实上我已经投了很多份简历了,但是仍没有回复。要不是为了挣钱养家,我会立刻辞了这份工作。

情景单词快记忆

tracer 绘图员	simultaneous 同时的
publisher 出版人员	graphic designer 美术设计员
journalist 记者	editor 编辑
interpreter 口译者	director 导演
talent 天才；人才	actress 女演员
photographer 摄影师	scholar 学者
translator 翻译家	novelist 小说家
playwright 剧作家	linguist 语言学家
economist 经济学家	chemist 化学家
composer 作曲家	designer 设计家；服装设计师
sculptor 雕刻家	

③ 跳槽 Job-hopping

高频单句大放送

01. Job-hopping is common in big cities.
    在大城市跳槽是常事。

02. She plans her job hopping.
    她在考虑跳槽。

03. There's no doubt that job-hopping has its draw-backs as well as merits.
    毫无疑问，跳槽有优点也有缺点。

04. Could job-hopping be good for you career?
    跳槽对你的职业生涯有益处吗？

05. Are you thinking of jumping ship?
    你在考虑跳槽吗？

06. Everyday we hear about people making radical career changes.
    每天我们都听说有人跳槽了。

07. She shifts to a well-known company.
    她跳槽去了一家很有名的公司。

08. Why do you want to change your job?
    你为什么想要换个工作？

09. When employees transfer jobs, they take business secrets, such as technical

data, customer lists and operational models with them.

员工跳槽时会带走商业秘密，比如技术数据、客户资料和公司运作模式。

10. We can not immediately conclude that the frequent transfer from one job to another undermines loyalty.

我们不能马上得出结论，频繁地跳槽降低了员工的忠诚度。

🔵 口语问答面对面

Jasmine: Kevin, there's something I want to talk to you about.

Kevin: Jasmine, why are you whispering?

茉莉: 凯文，我想跟你谈件事。

凯文: 茉莉，你干吗那么小声？

Jasmine: I've been talking to Web Tracker. I'm thinking of jumping ship.

Kevin: What? Are you serious? You'd defect to our archrival?

茉莉: 我一直跟"网络搜寻家"有联系。我在考虑跳槽。

凯文: 什么？你是认真的吗？你要向敌人投诚？

Jasmine: Why do you want to change your job?

Kevin: I want more challenges.

茉莉: 你为什么想要换个工作？

凯文: 我想要更多的挑战。

Jasmine: Keep your voice down. We'll talk more later. Right now I need to see Bessie.

Kevin: We definitely have to talk, Jasmine. And watch your back. Tony is still mad about his nose.

茉莉: 小声点。我们晚点再详谈。我现在要去找贝西。

凯文: 我们一定得聊聊，茉莉。多留点神，托尼还在气他鼻子的那档事。

Tina: How's your job at the state-owned enterprise?

Julia: Oh, I no longer work there. I'm working with a multinational corporation.

蒂娜: 你在那家国有企业工作得怎么样？

茱莉亚: 我已经不在那儿了，现在我在一家跨国公司上班。

Tina: You changed jobs again? Why do you move so frequently?

Julia: I want to try different things before I find the one I really like.

蒂娜: 你又换工作了？怎么跳得这么频繁呀？

茱莉亚: 我想试试不同的工作，然后看看到底喜欢哪个。

Tina: Why don't you stick with one job for a bit longer?

Julia: I could handle everything pretty well in the old position, so I decided to move around and learn something new.

蒂娜: 你怎么不在一个工作岗位上多做一段时间呢?

茉莉亚: 原来的工作我都能处理得很好, 所以我想换换环境, 学点新东西。

Tina: How's your current job going?

Julia: I'm pretty satisfied with it. I can broaden my experience, learn lots of new things, and have more development opportunities.

蒂娜: 现在这工作怎么样呀?

茉莉亚: 挺满意的。我可以拓宽视野, 学到很多新东西, 还能得到更多发展机会。

Tina: Sounds good, but I still think perhaps you should first have a clear career path to follow and then decide whether to change your job or not.

Julia: Yes, you're right. When I graduated, I didn't know what I really wanted to do or what I could do. Now things are growing much clearer.

蒂娜: 不错, 但我还是认为你该先找到一个明确的职业生涯发展道路, 然后再决定要不要换工作。

茉莉亚: 没错。刚毕业的时候, 我不知道自己想做什么, 也不知道自己能做什么, 现在我清楚多了。

Tina: Do you have a definite career path yet?

Julia: I'm not sure. I just like the job I'm doing now.

蒂娜: 现在有明确的职业生涯发展道路了吗?

茉莉亚: 还是不太清楚, 不过我还挺喜欢现在的工作的。

情景单词快记忆

universal education 普及教育

compulsory education/free education 义务教育

preschool education 学前教育

elementary education 初等教育

secondary education 中等教育

higher/tertiary education 高等教育

adult education 成人教育

teachers' college 师范学院

polytechnical university 工业大学

agricultural university 农业大学

medical university 医科大学

conservatory of music 音乐学院

academy of fine arts 美术学院

physical culture institute 体育学院

State Education Commission 国家教育委员会	television and radio broadcasting university 电视广播大学
institution of higher education 高等学校	night school for adults 成人夜校
university of liberal arts 文科大学	vocational school 职业学校
college/university of science and engineering 理工科大学	attached middle school 附中
normal university/teachers' university 师范大学	self-taught examination 自学考试

读书笔记

19 商务工作
Business Work

① 自主创业 Starting a Business

🔵 高频单句大放送

01. I'd like to take a loan out to open a business.
我想贷款创业。

02. I think I should start my own business.
我想我应该自己创业。

03. What kind of business will you start?
你想开什么样的公司？

04. What kind of business is your company?
你公司主营什么业务？

05. I need to hire some people for my business.
我需要为我的业务雇用一些人。

06. What financial steps do I need to take to open my own business?
我自己创业需要办理什么财务手续吗？

07. What should I name my business?
我应该怎样命名我的公司呢？

08. Why do you want to start your own business?
你为什么想自己创业？

09. I'd really like to start a shoe store.
我想开一个鞋店。

10. Well, after you've taken out the loan, you need to file with the city.
贷完款后需要在市里备案。

🔵 口语问答面对面

Tom: I really want to start my business.
Jane: What? Why?
汤姆: 我想开一家公司。
简: 什么？为什么呀？

Tom: Well, I've always wanted to have one, and I could work for myself.

Jane: Well, but that's a lot of hard work.

汤姆: 我一直想开一家公司，可以自己当老板。

简: 确实，但那是一项很艰难的工作。

Tom: I know, but I'm willing to do it.

Jane: Even take the loans and everything?

汤姆: 我知道，但是我很愿意去做。

简: 甚至要贷款还有其他很多事?

Jane: I think you should go for it. I believe in you.

Tom: Thanks. That means a lot. I think I will.

简: 我觉得你应该去做。我相信你。

汤姆: 谢谢，这对我来说很重要。我会努力的。

Jane: Most people who start their own business fail.

Tom: But he made a fortune by starting his own business.

简: 很多自己创业的人都失败了。

汤姆: 但他自己开公司却挣了不少钱。

Jane: How will you operate your company?

Tom: Well, I can work at home, saving the cost of renting an office.

简: 你打算怎样运营你的公司?

汤姆: 我可以在家里工作，省下租办公室的钱。

Jane: I want to start my own business rather than work as a senior employee.

Tom: That's an amazing idea! Go for it, man.

简: 我想自己创业而不是做个高级打工仔。

汤姆: 这真是一个很棒的想法! 去做吧，哥们儿!

Jane: She told me she wanted to start a company.

Tom: Oh, I always think she is smart enough to go into business.

简: 她告诉我她想开公司。

汤姆: 哦，我一直觉得她很聪明可以去经营。

Jane: Do you want to make your own phone company?

Tom: Yeah, I have had the idea for a long time.

简: 你想自己开一家电话公司吗?

汤姆: 是啊，我有这个想法已经很长时间了。

Jane: If I succeed in running this company, you can also come to help me.

Tom: Sure, I'll help you out whatever I can.

简: 如果我成功运作这个公司，你也可以过来帮我。

汤姆: 好的，我会尽我所能帮你的。

🔵 情景单词快记忆

angel investor 天使投资人	business plan 商业计划书
debt 债务	equipment 设备
financial statement 财务报表	growth 增长
human capital 人力资本	joint venture 合资
knowledge 知识	lender 贷款方
marketing 营销	name 名称
operation 运营	profit margins 利润率
quick restaurant delivery 快餐服务	regulation 规则
sales channel 销售渠道	tax 税务
venture capital 风险投资	website 网站
zeal 热情	

② 产品介绍 Presenting Products

🔵 高频单句大放送

01. Our products are of prime quality.
我们的产品质量一流。

02. Our new product is elegant and practical.
我们的新产品既大方又实用。

03. This type of our product is very popular in domestic market.
我们这一型号的新产品在国内非常受欢迎。

04. We have a wide selection of this product.
我们这类产品的式样齐全。

05. Our products have won a high admiration and are widely trusted at home and abroad.
我们的产品深受国内外客户的信赖和赞誉。

06. Our new varieties are introduced one after another.
我们新品迭出。

07. This product is famous for high-quality raw materials, full range of specifications and sizes, and great variety of designs and colours.
这一产品以优质原料、尺寸齐全、品种花样繁多而著称。

08. Quality is first, and consumers the highest.
质量第一，用户至上。

09. This coat is suitable for men and women of all ages in all seasons.
这一外套适合男女老幼四季穿着。

10. We hold the policy of bringing more convenience to the people in their daily life.
我们秉持方便顾客生活的方针。

🔵 口语问答面对面

Cathy: Ah, yes, this is the model I am interested in.
Black: I should be very happy to give you any further information you need on it.
凯西: 啊，是的，这就是我所感兴趣的那种样式。
布莱克: 我很乐意提供您所需要的关于它的进一步的信息。

Cathy: What are the specifications?
Black: If I may refer you to page eight of the brochure, you'll find all the specifications there.
凯西: 都有哪些规格呢?
布莱克: 如果您看一下手册的第 8 页，就会在那儿找到所有的规格。

Cathy: Now what about service life?
Black: Our tests indicate that this model has a service life of at least 50, 000 hours.
凯西: 关于使用寿命呢?
布莱克: 我们的实验表明这种样式至少可以使用 50000 小时。

Cathy: Is that an average figure for this type of equipment?
Black: Oh, no, far from it. That's about 50,000 hours longer than any other made in its price range.
凯西: 这是这种设备的平均数据吗?
布莱克: 不是的，相差还很远。这种比在它的价格范围内的任何其他样式都要高出 50000 小时左右。

Cathy: That's impressive. Now what happens if something goes wrong when we're using it?

Black: If that were to happen, just contact our nearest agent and they'll send someone round immediately.

凯西: 这一点给我印象颇深。不过如果这种设备在我们使用的时候发生故障, 该怎么办呢?

布莱克: 一旦发生那样的情况, 您可以同我们最近的办事处联系, 他们会马上派人过去的。

Cathy: Do you offer discounts for regular purchases?

Black: Yes, we do indeed. Our usual figure is around 5%, but that depends on the size of the order.

凯西: 长期购买, 你们提供折扣吗?

布莱克: 是的, 我们确实这样做。通常的数目是 5% 左右, 但那还要根据订货的多少来定。

Cathy: Yes, of course. Well, thank you very much, Mr. Black.

Black: Not at all, I hope we shall be hearing from you very shortly.

凯西: 那当然了。好了, 非常感谢, 布莱克先生。

布莱克: 不客气。希望尽快听到您的消息。

Cathy: Do you have some samples you could show me?

Black: Yeah, this way, please.

凯西: 你有没有样品可以给我看一下?

布莱克: 当然有了, 这边请。

Cathy: What about having a look at sample first?

Black: No, thank you.

凯西: 先看一看样品吧?

布莱克: 不用了, 谢谢。

Cathy: Are you interested in my products?

Black: Yeah, please outline the characteristics of your products first.

凯西: 你对我们的产品感兴趣吗?

布莱克: 是的, 请先简略说明你们产品的特性。

情景单词快记忆

selected material 用料上乘	superior material 优质原料
perfect in workmanship 做工精细	skillful manufacture 制作精巧
sophisticated technology 工艺精良	latest technology 最新工艺
finely processed 加工精细	modern design 造型新颖
professional design 设计合理	durable in use 经久耐用
attractive design 款式新颖	various styles 款式齐全
elegant shape 式样优雅	fashionable pattern 花色入时
color brilliancy 色泽光润	complete in specifications 规格齐全
delicate color 色泽素雅	pure whiteness 洁白纯正
superior quality 质量上乘	reliable reputation 信誉可靠
reliable quality 质量可靠	wide varieties 品种繁多

③ 产品质量 Product Quality

高频单句大放送

01. Could we check these samples?
我们能检测一下样品吗?

02. The quality of the products we ordered is in accordance with the catalogue.
我们订的产品质量和目录中的一样。

03. The order this time doesn't work out too well.
这次订的货使用效果不佳。

04. The goods are available in different qualities.
此货有多种不同的质量可供。

05. They are fully qualified to pass opinions on the quality of this merchandise.
他们完全有资格对这种产品的质量发表意见。

06. The quality is all right, but the style is a bit out-dated.
质量无问题, 只是式样有点过时。

07. Our Certificate of Quality is made valid by means of the official seal.
我们的质量证明书盖公章方为有效。

08. As long as the quality is good, it hardly matters if the price is a little bit higher.
只要能保证质量, 售价高点都无所谓。

09. We sincerely hope the quality is in conformity with the contract stipulations.

我们真诚希望质量与合同规定相符。

10. Our quality is based solely on our sales samples.
    我们的质量完全以货样为准。

口语问答面对面

Cathy: I can promise you that, if you buy our product, you will be getting quality.

Eric: I've looked at your units, and I am very happy with them. Your goods are all far above standard quality.

凯西: 我可以向你保证。如果你买了我们的产品，你会得到好品质。

艾瑞克: 我看过你们的单件，我很满意。你们的商品质量高过标准质量。

Cathy: We spend a lot of money to make sure that our quality is much better. We don't sacrifice quality for quick profits.

Eric: Well, we're really interested in placing an order under negotiation. We can start the negotiations as soon as you want.

凯西: 我们投入了大量的资金来确保质量一流。我们不会为了即期利润而有损质量。

艾瑞克: 是的。我方真的很愿意谈判后就订货。你们想谈判的话我们随时都可以。

Cathy: I'm glad we'll be able to do business together. I'll have some quotes ready for you by tomorrow morning.

Eric: Fine. Also, would you mind if I asked to see a surveyor's report of your products? I may have a few more questions about your quality analysis.

凯西: 我很高兴我们能在一起做生意。到明天早晨我方将为您准备好一些报价单。

艾瑞克: 很好。还有，您不介意我要求看一下你方产品的检查报告吧？对你们的质量分析我可能还有一些问题。

Cathy: How do you feel like the quality of our products.

Eric: Just alright. I think they are a little thin.

凯西: 你觉得我们产品的质量怎么样？

艾瑞克: 还行吧，我觉得稍微有点儿薄。

Cathy: The curtains are beautiful for their novel designs and elegant colors.

Eric: Yeah. I think they will find a good market in my market.

凯西: 这些窗帘图案新颖，色调雅致。

艾瑞克: 是的。我认为它在我国市场上能畅销。

Cathy: Two boxes of your product didn't coincide with your sample last time.

Eric: I don't know what is happening. There haven't been such things with us. Maybe the factory sent wrong boxes.

凯西: 上次你们的货物中有两箱与样品不符。

艾瑞克: 这是怎么回事。我们从来没发生过这样的事情。也许是工厂方面送错了箱子。

Cathy: Here is what differs from your sample.

Eric: I got it. I am contacting the factory right now.

凯西: 这是与你们样品不符的东西。

艾瑞克: 我明白了。我马上和厂家联系。

Cathy: I want to have your opinion on the quality problem of the goods.

Eric: We regret for this, but we guarantee there is nothing wrong with our products.

凯西: 我想听听贵方对这次货物质量问题的看法。

艾瑞克: 出现这样的事情我们感到很遗憾。但是，我们敢保证产品本身质量没有问题。

Cathy: That means we should ask for compensation from the insurance agent.

Eric: I think so.

凯西: 就是说要我们向保险公司要求索赔了。

艾瑞克: 我认为应该是这样。

Cathy: We will not get to the bottom since this is the first claim.

Eric: There won't be such things.

凯西: 这次是第一次出现问题，所以我们不再深究了。

艾瑞克: 以后不会再出现类似的情况了。

🔵 情景单词快记忆

QE (quality engineer) 质量工程师	certification 认证
QA (quality assurance) 质量保证	certification system 认证体系
QC (quality control) 质量控制	certification body 认证机构
IC (incomming quality control) 进料检验	inspection body 检验机构
FQC (finished quality control) 成品检验	license 许可证
OQC (outgoing quality control) 出货检验	certificate of conformity 合格证书
product specification 产品规范	approval 批准

20 贸易详情
Trade Details

① 报价 Offer

高频单句大放送

01. We would like to modify our offer of August 25.
本公司希望修改 8 月 25 日的报价。

02. We reinstate our offer dated November 10.
我方恢复 11 月 10 日的报盘。

03. We can offer you a quotation based upon the international market.
我们可以按国际市场价格给您报价。

04. Please renew your offer for two days further.
请将报盘延期两天。

05. As recently the goods are in extremely short supply, we regret being unable to offer the price.
近来货源很紧，因此很抱歉我们不能报盘。

06. We are pleased to quote you for the goods as follows.
兹就该商品向贵方报价如下。

07. My offer was based on reasonable profit, not on wild speculations.
我的报价以合理利润为依据，不是漫天要价。

08. Here is out latest CIF price.
这是我们最新的到岸价。

09. Please note that the prices of the commodities will change with seasons.
请注意，商品的价格会随着季节变化。

10. The present price fluctuation in the world market has forced us to adjust our price accordingly.
目前国际市场价格变化不定，迫使我们必须相应地调整价格。

口语问答面对面

Hugh: Could you make offers for the items listed in your catalog?
Larry: Yes. Here is the price list. But the prices are subject to our final confirmation.

休: 目录中所列的商品你们能报价吗?

拉里: 能。这是价格单, 但是这些价格以我方最后的确认为准。

Larry: What's the quantity you're likely to take?

Hugh: 200 tons for a start.

拉里: 你想要订多少?

休: 先订 200 吨。

Larry: And the port of destination?

Hugh: Washington.

拉里: 目的港是哪里?

休: 华盛顿。

Hugh: How long will you leave your offer open?

Larry: It's valid for seven days. Your early reply will be highly appreciated.

休: 报价有效期多长?

拉里: 有效期为 7 天。尽早回复, 我们将不胜感激。

Larry: How soon do you want the goods to be delivered?

Hugh: Early April.

拉里: 什么时候要货?

休: 4 月初。

Larry: Did you receive our inquiry sheets yet?

Hugh: Yes, and I'm checking it out.

拉里: 你收到我们的询价单了吗?

休: 收到了, 我正在看。

Larry: I'm sorry to say that the price you quote is too high.

Hugh: We have done a lot of business with other customers at this price.

拉里: 我很遗憾你们报价太高了。

休: 我们按这个价已经和其他客户做了大批生意。

Larry: Would it be possible to lower the price any?

Hugh: While we appreciate your cooperation, we regret to say that we can't reduce our price any further.

拉里: 价钱能便宜点吗?

休: 虽然我们感谢贵方的合作, 但是很抱歉, 我们不能再降价了。

Larry: I understand all your prices are on CIF basis. We'd rather have you quote us FOB price.

Hugh: Okay, we'll let you know the FOB price as soon as possible.

拉里: 你方报的是到岸价，希望能给我们报离岸价。

休: 好的，我们会尽快告知你离岸价的。

Larry: When can I have your firm CIF price, that is to say, the final offer?

Hugh: We'll have it worked out by this evening and let you have it tomorrow morning.

拉里: 我什么时候能得到你们公司的实盘到案价格，也就是说，最后的报价？

休: 我们将在今晚制定出来，明天早上就可以给你了。

情景单词快记忆

price term 价格条款	FCB plane 飞机离岸价
FOB (free on board) 离岸价格	acceptable 可以接受的；可以使用的
CIF (cost insurance and freight) 到岸价格	FOR (free on rail) 火车交货价
C&F (cost and freight) 离岸加运费价格	FOT (free on truck) 汽车交货价
FOB liner terms FOB 班轮条件	FAS (free alongside ship) 船边交货价
FOB stowed 船上交货并理舱	ex factory 工厂交货价
FOB trimmed 船上交货并平舱	ex plantation 农场交货价
FOB under tackle FOB 吊钩下交货	ex warehouse 仓库交货价
CIF liner terms CIF 班轮条件	price contract 价格合约
CIF ex ship's hold CIF 舱底交货	price per unit 单价

② 订货 Ordering Goods

高频单句大放送

01. We regret that we are not in a position to meet your requirements as for the time being goods have been fully booked.
很遗憾，因货已售罄，目前很难满足你方需求。

02. I hope this order is followed by many other orders.
我希望这个订单的后面还跟着许多订单。

03. We are inclined to place large orders with you.

我们想向你们大量订购。

04. I regret that I have to notify you of one order being cancelled.
非常遗憾，我方不得不通知贵方有一个订单需要取消。

05. We'll send our official order today.
我们今天会寄上正式的订单。

06. We don't have any stock of the bicycles as you required.
我们没有你要的那种自行车现货。

07. If I place an order now, when would you be able to ship it?
如果现在下单子，什么时候可以出货？

08. Can you accept this order? It's not a big one.
你们能否接受这份订单？数量不大。

09. Will you accept special order?
你们接受特殊订单吗？

10. What's the minimum quantity of an order for your goods?
你们订货的最低量是多少？

口语问答面对面

Buyer: I'd like to order 500 pairs of Rainbow socks.
Seller: Rainbow socks are one of our best selling goods. They are out of stock at the moment.
买方: 我想订 500 双彩虹牌袜子。
卖方: 彩虹牌袜子是我们这里卖得最好的产品，现在暂时缺货。

Buyer: Are you expecting any to come in soon?
Seller: We expect to have them back in stock around May 10. However, we can provide you with another brand of similar quality.
买方: 会很快进货吗？
卖方: 我们预计在 5 月 10 号左右进货。不过，我们可以向您提供同样质量的另一种牌子的袜子。

Buyer: What's the brand?
Seller: It's Sunflower, also one of our best-selling goods, which we can sell for as low as $1.5 each.
买方: 是什么牌子的？
卖方: 向日葵牌，这也是我们的一个畅销货品。我们开价很低，每双 1.5 美元。

Buyer: I'd like to place a trial order for the Sunflower socks then.

Seller: That's fine.

买方: 我订购一些向日葵牌袜子作为试单吧。

卖方: 好的。

Seller: How many would you like to order?

Buyer: 300. If the goods sell as well as we expect, we will send further orders in the near future.

卖方: 您要订多少?

买方: 300 双。如果货物的销售情况像我们预期的一样好，我们不久还会继续订购。

Buyer: Please prepare the sales contract. After signing the contract, we will apply for an L/C in your favor.

Seller: OK, I will prepare the sales contract as soon as we can.

买方: 请准备好销售合同。在签订好合同之后，我们将申请开出以你为受益人的信用证。

卖方: 好的，我会尽快准备发合同的。

Seller: How much did you want to increase your order?

Buyer: We need three times as much as we originally ordered.

卖方: 你们的订单要增加多少?

买方: 我们需要原来订单的三倍订购量。

Buyer: I'd like to order some paper.

Seller: Sure, what package would you like to go with?

买方: 我想订购一些纸。

卖方: 好的。你想要哪种交易套餐?

Buyer: We need to make a change on our last order.

Seller: Sure. Do you know the order number?

买方: 上回的订单我们需要更改一下。

卖方: 好的。你知道订单号吗?

Buyer: We should be glad if you would accept our order for shoes whose number is NO. 1203.

Seller: We regret that we are unable to meet your requirement for the time being as goods have been full booked.

卖方: 如果贵公司能够接受 1203 编号的鞋子订单，我们将很高兴。

买方: 因为订单已满，我们很遗憾目前不能满足你方要求。

情景单词快记忆

to place an order in blank 寄空白订单	to repeat an order 继续订货
to take an order 订货	to cancel an order 取消订货；撤销订单
to accept an order/to take an order 接受订单；接受订货	to confirm an order 确认订货
to close an order 决定成交	to book an order 已将订货列账
to fill an order/to put an order through 执行订单	to increase an order 增加订货
to complete an order 完成订货	to reduce an order 减少订货
to send an order 寄送一份订单	to solicit an order 请求订货
to dispatch an order 发货；寄出货品	to miss an order 错过一次订货
to ship an order 装船；已装船	charges 费用
to modify an order 改变订货；变更订单	

③ 签订合同 Signing a Contract

高频单句大放送

01. How do you think if we make a 2- year contract?
我们签订一个有效期为 2 年的合同你认为怎么样？

02. It's necessary to check the contract closely before you sign.
在签合同之前应该仔细检查一下合同。

03. The contract shall be valid for 20 years from the effective date of the contract.
本合同有效期从合同生效之日算起共 20 年。

04. The contract is made out in Chinese and English languages in duplicate.
本合同用英文和中文两种文字写成，一式两份。

05. We signed a contract for cotton.
我们签订了一份棉花合同。

06. Do we always make a contract for every deal?
每笔交易都需要订一份合同吗？

07. An American company and Sinopec have entered into a new contract.
中国石化公司已经和美国一家公司签订了一份新合同。

08. One party cannot cancel the contract without first securing the other one's agreement.
如果没有事先征得一方的同意，另一方不能取消合同。

09. Once the contract is permitted by the Japanese government, it is legally binding upon both parties.

合同一经日本政府批准，对双方就有了法律约束力。

10. The contract will come into force when it is signed by both parties.

合同一经双方签订即生效。

🌐 口语问答面对面

Buyer: There is something I want to ask you about Clause 6.

Seller: Yes, please.

买方: 我想问你有关第六条款的事。

卖方: 请问吧。

Buyer: Could we revise the contract tomorrow?

Seller: Yes, of course.

买方: 我们明天可以修改合同吗？

卖方: 当然可以。

Buyer: We expect to have a final contract ready in a week.

Seller: OK.

买方: 我们希望能在一星期内准备好最终的合同。

卖方: 好的。

Buyer: Can we meet halfway on this?

Seller: Then it's settled.

买方: 我们能否各让一半?

卖方: 就这样定了。

Buyer: Shall we sign the contract now?

Seller: Yes. Everything is settled. Let's begin.

买方: 我们现在就签约吗？

卖方: 是的。一切就绪。我们开始吧。

Lawyer: I made a very close study of the draft contract last night.

Client: Any questions?

律师: 昨晚我仔细审阅了合同草案。

委托人: 有什么问题吗?

Buyer: Before I sign off, I have to ask my attorney to read it over.

Seller: That's fine.
买方: 在我签字之前，我得让我的律师把整份合约看一遍。
卖方: 可以。

Buyer: What's the term of this contract?
Seller: It's two years and upon its expiration it will be renewed every two years subject to agreement of both parties.
买方: 这个合同的期限是多长?
卖方: 这是两年期限，期满时，会根据双方的协议，每两年重订一次。

Buyer: This contract will run for one year of the trial period.
Seller: That's reasonable.
买方: 这个合同将有 1 年的试用期。
卖方: 很合理。

Buyer: Would you mind if we make a 5-year contract?
Seller: No, not at all.
买方: 我们签署一个有效期为 5 年的合同好吗?
卖方: 好的，当然可以。

情景单词快记忆

contract 合同；订立合同	to land a contract 得到（拥有）合同
contractor 订约人；承包人	to countersign a contract 会签合同
contractual 合同的；契约的	to repeat a contract 重复合同
to make a contract 签订合同	an executory contract 尚待执行的合同
to place a contract 订合同	a nice fat contract 一个很有利的合同
to enter into a contract 订合同	originals of the contract 合同正本
to sign a contract 签合同	copies of the contract 合同副本
to draw up a contract 拟订合同	a written contract 书面合同
to draft a contract 起草合同	to make some concession 做某些让步
to get a contract 得到合同	trial period 试用期

21 贸易往来
Trade Contacts

① 保险 Insurance

高频单句大放送

01. What is the insurance premium?
保险费是多少？

02. An All Risks policy covers every sort of hazard, doesn't it?
一份综合险保单保所有的险，是吗？

03. TheF.P.A. policy only covers you against total loss in the case of minor perils.
平安险只有在发生较小危险时才给保全部损失险。

04. The F.P.A. doesn't cover partial loss of the nature of particular average.
平安险不包括单独海损性质的部分损失。

05. We can serve you with a broad range of coverage against all kinds of risks for sea transport.
我公司可以承保海洋运输的所有险别。

06. Are there any other clauses in marine policies?
海运险还包括其他条款吗？

07. The risk of breakage is covered by marine insurance, isn't it?
破碎险是包括在海洋运输货物险之内的，对吗？

08. Please fill in the application form.
请填写一下保单。

09. What kind of insurance are you able to provide for my consignment?
贵公司能为我们这批货保哪些险呢？

10. What insurance will you take out?
你们打算投保哪些险？

口语问答面对面

Helen: I'm calling to discuss the level of insurance coverage you've requested for your order.

Henry: I believe that we have requested an amount of twenty-five percent above the invoice value.

海伦: 我打电话来是想讨论你所要求的订单保险额的级别。

亨利: 我想我们要求的是高于发票价值百分之二十五的保险金额。

Helen: Yes, that's right. We have no problem in complying with your request, but we think that the amount is a bit excessive.

Henry: We've had a lot of trouble in the past with damaged goods.

海伦: 是的，没错。我们可以答应这个要求，但是我们觉得金额有点太高。

亨利: 我们过去有太多货物毁损的困扰。

Helen: I can understand your concern. However, the normal coverage for goods of this type is to insure them for the total invoice amount plus ten percent.

Henry: We would feel more comfortable with the additional protection.

海伦: 我能了解你的考虑。然而，一般这类产品的保险额度是发票总额再加百分之十。

亨利: 有额外的保障会让我们觉得安全些。

Helen: Unfortunately, if you want to increase the coverage, we will have to charge you extra for the additional cost.

Henry: But the insurance was supposed to be included in the quotation.

海伦: 很遗憾，如果你们想增加保险额的话，我们就得向你们收取额外的费用。

亨利: 但是保险应该包含在报价里了。

Helen: We can, however, arrange the extra coverage. But I suggest you contact your insurance agent there and compare rates.

Henry: You're right. It might be cheaper on this end.

海伦: 不过，超出的保险额我们可以再商量。但是我建议你和你们那边的保险代理商联络并比较一下价格。

亨利: 你说得没错，在这边可能会比较便宜。

Helen: What is the insurance premium?

Henry: The premium varies with the range of insurance.

海伦: 保险费是多少?

亨利: 保险费根据投保范围的大小而有所不同。

Helen: Yes, but we quoted you normal coverage at regular rates.

Henry: I see.

海伦: 是的，但是我们向你们报的价是一般比例下的正常保险额。

亨利: 我了解。

Helen: How long are the goods insured?

Henry: For 6 months.

海伦: 这些货保险期多长?

亨利: 6个月。

Helen: Are buyers responsible for the extra premium?

Henry: Yes. This is convention.

海伦: 由买方来负担额外的保险费吗?

亨利: 是的。这是惯例。

Helen: When shall we be able to get compensation from the insurance company?

Henry: As soon as we are through all the formalities.

海伦: 我们什么时候能够得到保险公司的补偿金呢?

亨利: 我们一切手续完成后就可以。

情景单词快记忆

acceptance policy 核保政策	accounting period 结算期
aggregated loss 累积损失	catastrophe risk 巨灾风险
cover 承保；责任额	rating 费率
deposit premium 预付保费	event limit 事件限额
excess loss 超额赔款	full coverage 全额承保
individual loss 单一损失	insurability 可保性
insured loss 保险损失	liability 责任
loading 附加费	loss occurrence 损失发生
loss participation 分担损失	loss settlement 损失赔付
premium 保费	priority 自负责任

② 佣金 Commission

高频单句大放送

01. What about the commission?
佣金是多少?

02. You can get a higher commission rate if you order a bigger quantity.
如果你们订货量大,佣金率就会高。

03. We don't pay any commission on our traditional products.
对我们的传统产品概不支付佣金。

04. Commission is allowed to agents only.
我们只对代理付佣金。

05. Is it possible to increase the commission to 4%?
能不能将佣金提高到 4% 呢?

06. You can grant us an extra commission of 2% to cover the additional risk.
你们可以获得另外 2% 的佣金,以补偿你们受的额外风险。

07. We can't agree to increase the rate of commission.
我们不能同意增加佣金率。

08. A 5% commission means an increase in our price.
5% 的佣金就等于价格提高了。

09. A 4% commission is the maximum.
我们最多给 4% 的佣金。

10. Is it possible to increase the commission to 4%?
能不能把佣金提高到 4% 呢?

口语问答面对面

Jennifer: William, what I'd like to bring up for discuss is the commission.
William: Well, Jennifer, you know, our prices are quoted on FOB net basis. As a rule, we don't allow any commission.
珍尼弗: 威廉,我想谈谈佣金问题。
威廉: 珍尼弗,你知道,我们报的是 FOB 净价。按惯例是不给佣金的。

Jennifer: But, you know, we're commission agent. We do business on commission basis. Commission transaction will surely help to push the sale of your products.
William: But your order is really not a large one.
珍尼弗: 可是,你知道,我们是佣金代理商。我们佣金代理商靠获得佣金来做生意。

带佣金贸易有助于你们产品的推销。

威廉: 可是你们的订单数目太小了。

Jennifer: What do you mean by a large one?

William: I mean that we'll consider giving some commission only when the order exceeds a total amount of \$50,000 or over.

珍尼弗: 那么你认为的大数目是多少呢？

威廉: 至少订单总额达到 50000 美元或以上，我们可以考虑给予你们一定的佣金。

Jennifer: It's really impossible for us to make any concession by allowing you any commission.

William: I'm sorry to hear that. But it doesn't matter and we can cooperate next time.

珍尼弗: 在给你们的佣金问题上，我们真的不可能作出任何让步了。

威廉: 听到这个消息我很遗憾。不过没关系，我们可以下次合作。

Jennifer: We would like to allow you another 2% commission for further promotion of our products.

William: To be frank with you, a commission of 2% wouldn't help very much.

珍尼弗: 我们愿再给你方 2% 的佣金，以进一步推销我们的产品。

威廉: 坦率地说，2% 的佣金帮助不大。

Jennifer: How large is the commission for this deal?

William: We will give you a 6% commission on every transaction.

珍尼弗: 这笔交易的佣金是多少？

威廉: 每笔交易我们将给你 6% 的佣金。

Jennifer: From other suppliers, we get a higher commission rate for the business in this line.

William: We'll allow you a higher commission rate if your sales score a substantial increase.

珍尼弗: 对这类产品的交易，我们从其他供货者那里可得到更高的佣金。

威廉: 如果你们的销量大幅度增长，我们会给予更高的佣金。

Jennifer: No further discussion?

William: I'm sorry, Jennifer. Please make allowance for our difficulties.

珍尼弗: 再没有商量的余地了？

威廉: 非常抱歉，珍尼弗。请谅解我们的难处。

William: Well, Jennifer, what do you think of this: you increase your order to $45,000 and we offer you 3% commission?

Jennifer: William, I very much appreciate your concession. But we can usually get 5% commission from European suppliers.

威廉: 好啊，珍尼弗，你觉得这样如何，如果你的订货总额在 45000 美元以上，我们可以考虑给予你们 3% 的佣金。

珍尼弗: 威廉，我很感谢你的让步。可是我们通常可以从欧洲供货商那里得到 5% 的佣金。

William: How much commission will you give?

Jennifer: Usually we give a 2% commission to the agent.

威廉: 你方愿意给多少佣金？

珍尼弗: 通常我们给代理商 2% 的佣金。

情景单词快记忆

commission (com.) 佣金；手续费	commission for collection 代收账款佣金
two or several items of commission 两笔或几笔佣金	commission insurance 佣金保险
all commissions 所有佣金	commission system 佣金制
commission transaction 付佣金的交易	commission agency 代理贸易
commission agent 代理商；代办人；代理贸易商	selling commission 代销佣金
commission charge 佣金；手续费	buying commission 代购佣金
overriding commission 追加佣金	rate of commission or scale of commission 佣金率
commission on a sliding scale 递加佣金	to pay the commission 支付佣金
commissions earned 佣金收入	present commission 现有佣金
commissions received in advance 预收佣金	three items of commission 三笔佣金

③ 纳税 Taxation

高频单句大放送

01. I need the tax form before two o'clock.
我两点前需要税单。

02. It pays to be honest with the taxman.
纳税诚实不吃亏。

03. The law obliges us to pay taxes.
法律使我们赋有纳税的义务。

04. Have you anything to declare?
你有什么要申报纳税的吗？

05. Failure to pay your taxes will make you liable to prosecution.
不缴纳税款就可能被起诉。

06. There are good economic reasons for using the income tax as a major source of revenue.
使用所得税作为财政收入主要来源有很好的经济原因。

07. It is correct to pay the modern individual income tax.
缴付现代的个人所得税是正确的。

08. Taxation is a powerful and essential economic instrument for a modern industrial economy.
税收是现代工业化经济的有力而必要的经济手段。

09. It's my lawyer who prepared my tax return.
我的律师帮我办理纳税。

10. The tax authorities try every means to prevent people from tax evasion.
税务机关采取各种办法防止逃税。

🔵 口语问答面对面

Taxpayer: My company will begin business soon, but I have little knowledge about the business tax. Can you introduce it?

Tax official: I will try my best. Generally speaking, the business tax is levied on the taxable service, the transfer of intangible asset and sale of the immovable property within China.

纳税人：我公司马上就要营业了，但我对营业税知之甚少，能介绍一下营业税的知识吗？

税务局：尽我所能吧！一般地说，在中国提供应税业务、转让无形资产和出卖不动产都要缴纳营业税。

Taxpayer: What do you mean by the taxable services?

Tax official: They are the definite items stipulated by the law, such as the transportation, construction, finance, insurance, etc. They do not include the processing, repairs and replacement services for they are subject to the value added tax.

纳税人: 什么是应税业务?

税务局: 税法有明确的规定。比如交通运输、建筑安装、金融、保险等。不包括加工、修理、修配业务,因为它们要缴增值税。

Taxpayer: It is easy to understand the immovable property, but what do you mean by the intangible asset?

Tax official: It means the royalties include patent right, proprietary technology, copy right, trademark right and so on.

纳税人: 不动产好理解,无形资产指什么?

税务局: 指各种专有权,如专利权、专有技术、版权、商标权等。

Taxpayer: What about the tax base?

Tax official: In most cases, it is the total consideration received, including additional fees and charges.

纳税人: 计税收入如何确定?

税务局: 大多数情况下指全部价款包括价外费用。

Taxpayer: Does that include the turnover received in advance?

Tax official: Yes, it does in the case of transfer of the intangible assets or immovable property.

纳税人: 预收的价款也计算在内吗?

税务局: 是的,对于无形资产和不动产是这样。

A: All these commodities are duty free.

B: Wow, this is a good news to us.

A: 所有这些商品都免征关税。

B: 哇,这对我们来说是个好消息。

A: Is it possible to gain exemption from tariff?

B: Yes, but you need official documents.

A: 有没有可能免除关税?

B: 可以,但是你需要官方文件。

A: How mush is my tariff?

B: It's going to be $5,623.

A: 我的关税是多少?

B: 5623 美元。

A: Will we have to pay tariff on our imports?
B: Yeah, all imports must be declared to customs.
A: 我们要交进口税吗?
B: 是的，所有进口货物必须报关。

A: We can't ship the goods without paying duty.
B: But we are responsible for the charges including custom duties on export.
A: 不缴税的话我们不能运送这些货物。
B: 可是我们负担的费用包括出口关税啊。

情景单词快记忆

State Administration of Taxation 国家税务总局	tax avoidance 避税
local taxation bureau 地方税务局	tax evasion 逃税
business tax 营业税	tax base 税基
individual income tax 个人所得税	refund after collection 先征后退
income tax for enterprises 企业所得税	withhold and remit tax 代扣代缴
tax returns filing 纳税申报	collect and remit tax 代收代缴
taxes payable 应交税金	income from authors remuneration 稿酬所得
the assessable period for tax payment 纳税期限	tax year 纳税年度
consolidate reporting 合并申报	state treasury 国库
tax inspection report 纳税检查报告	tax preference 税收优惠

读书笔记

22 商务活动 Business Activities

① 产品推销 Product Promotion

🔵 高频单句大放送

01. If you are really interested in our products, we can talk about the price in details.
如果您确实对我们的产品感兴趣，我们可以详细地谈谈价格。

02. The prices are subject to our final confirmation.
这些价格以我们的最后确认为准。

03. This price is quite reasonable.
这个价钱是非常合理的。

04. Don't you want to look at some rings?
您不想看看戒指吗？

05. This TV set is on sale.
这款电视正在减价销售。

06. This air-conditioner is the best seller of this year.
这款空调是今年最畅销的。

07. These are the latest styles in shoes.
这些都是最新款式的鞋。

08. This pair is of our best quality.
这双是我们这儿质地最好的了。

09. How do you feel?
您感觉怎么样？

10. This refrigerator is of low noise design.
这款冰箱是低噪声设计。

🔵 口语问答面对面

A: May I see the general manager?
B: I'm afraid he is not in. Is there anything I can do for you?
A: 我能见一下总经理吗？
B: 恐怕他不在。我可以为您效劳吗？

A: If you are really interested in our products, we can talk about the price in details.

B: That's good.

A: 如果您确实对我们的产品感兴趣，我们可以详细地谈谈价格。

B: 好的。

A: The prices are subject to our final confirmation.

B: Okay.

A: 这些价格以我们的最后确认为准。

B: 好的。

A: May I have an indication of price? Can I have your price sheet?

B: Yes, of course.

A: 我可以问一下价格吗? 你能给我一份价目表吗?

B: 当然可以。

A: I'll send your catalogues to those who are interested.

B: Thanks a lot.

A: 我会把你们的产品目录转交给感兴趣的人的。

B: 非常感谢。

A: How long will it take to deliver the orders?

B: One month at most.

A: 你们多长时间可以交货?

B: 最多一个月。

A: I'm sorry I don't like the cell phone in such color.

B: But, believe it or not, this color will be really po-pular in this season.

A: 抱歉我不喜欢这种颜色的手机。

B: 但是不管您喜不喜欢，这种颜色在这一季节会很受欢迎。

A: Really?

B: Yes. So far, we've got a lot of orders of cell phone in this color.

A: 真的吗?

B: 是的。到目前为止，我们已经接到了很多这个颜色手机的订单。

A: You look graceful with this pearl necklace.

B: Really?

A: 您带这款珍珠项链看起来很高雅。

B: 真的吗?

A: I'd like to buy this one, but it's a little expensive.
B: I've already quoted you the bottom price.
A: 我想买这个，但是价格有点儿贵。
B: 我已经给您报了最低价了。

情景单词快记忆

salable 畅销的	popular 有销路的
find a market 销售	selling line 销路
trial sale/test sale/test market 试销	salable goods 畅销货
popular goods 快销货	the best selling line (the best seller) 热门货
to find (have) a ready market 有销路；畅销	to have a strong footing in a market 很有销路
good market 畅销	poor(no) market 滞销
goods that sell well 畅销货	sell like wild fire 畅销；销得很快
selling technique 推销技术	selling and administrative expense 推销及管理费用
selling concept 推销观点	selling 卖的；出售的；销路好的
sell 卖；销售；有销路	sales agent 代销人；销售代理商
sell at a bargain/sell at a profit 廉价出售	sell goods at a high figure 高价出售
predatory dumping 掠夺性倾销	International Dumping Code 国际反倾销法
marketing system 销售体系	a company's marketing program 一家公司的销售计划
sales promotion 促销	marketing strategy 销售策略
market segmentation 市场分割	selling cost 销售成本
selling expense 销售费用	selling operation 销售业务
selling profit 销售利润	

② 商展 Trade Fair

高频单句大放送

01. Are all the components made in Taiwan?
　　零件全都是台湾制造的吗?

02. Would you like a packet of our promotional literature?
您要看看我们的宣传资料包吗?

03. I see your computer is fully IBM compatible.
我发现你的电脑可以和 IBM 完全相容。

04. Would you be interested in talking with him about our ideas for upcoming models?
您是否有兴趣与他谈论有关即将到来的模型?

05. I'm sure we can arrange it before then.
我相信我们可以在那之前安排好。

06. May I ask what company you work for?
可以问一下您服务于哪个公司吗?

07. May I help you?
需要帮忙吗?

08. I'd be glad to help.
很高兴能帮助您。

09. I represent Reese Computer and Supply Company.
我是李斯电脑供应公司的代表。

10. We do some subcontracting, but only in Taiwan.
我们只在台湾做一些分包。

口语问答面对面

Salesman: Good morning. May I help you?

Importer: I wonder if you can give me more information about this computer model you're showing?

推销员: 早上好，需要帮忙吗?

进口商: 我想你可不可以给我更多有关你们正在展示的这台计算机模型的信息呢?

Salesman: Would you like a packet of our promotional literature?

Importer: Thank you. I see your computer is fully IBM compatible.

推销员: 给您看看我们的宣传资料包怎么样?

进口商: 谢谢。我发现你的电脑可以与 IBM 完全相容。

Salesman: This model can run any software or DOS program.

Importer: These models seem to be quite small.

推销员: 这个模型能运行所有的软件、DOS 程序。

进口商: 这些模型看起来很小。

Salesman: One of the problems our company was trying to solve was to do away with the bulk of IBM desktops and their clones when we worked on this model. Our computer is only 11 pounds.

Importer: Remarkable! There's nothing quite like seeing a problem and solving it to create a good product.

推销员: 当我们研发这一模型时，我们公司尽力解决的问题就是废除大量 IBM 台式电脑以及对它们的克隆。我们的电脑只有 11 磅。

进口商: 了不起! 没有什么能比看到问题并解决它从而创建一个好产品更好的了。

Importer: Are all the components made here?

Salesman: Yes These computers are made here.

进口商: 零部件全都是这儿制造的吗?

推销员: 是的。这些电脑是在这生产的。

Importer: May I ask what company you work for?

Salesman: I represent Reese Computer and Supply Company. We're a high-volume, discount mail-order house.

进口商: 请问您服务于哪家公司呢?

推销员: 我是李斯电脑供应公司的代表，我公司是大规模的折扣邮购公司。

Salesman: Would you like to tour our factory and perhaps, even one or two of our subcontractors?

Importer: Yes, if it wouldn't take too long to arrange. I'm due to fly back to the States on Friday.

推销员: 您想参观我们的工厂以及一两个分包商吗?

进口商: 若不会花太多时间安排的话，我很乐意。我预订星期五乘机回美国。

Salesman: I'm sure we can arrange it before then. How about meeting the founder of our company? Would you be interested in talking with him about our ideas for upcoming models?

Importer: Yes, I think that would be useful. Thank you for your help.

推销员: 我保证能在那之前完成。见见我们公司的创办人怎么样? 您是否有兴趣和他谈论有关即将面世的这一模型?

进口商: 是的，我认为那很有用。谢谢您帮忙。

A: What's the date of the trade show?

B: From Oct.2 to Nov. 2.

A: 商展的日期是几号?

B: 从10月2号到11月2号。

A: Have you prepared the guidebook?

B: Yes.

A: 手册准备好了吗?

B: 准备好了。

🔵 情景单词快记忆

shareholder/stockholder 股票持有人；股东	dividend 股息；红利
cash dividend 现金配股	stock investment 股票投资
investment trust 投资信托	stock-jobber 股票经纪人
stock company 证券公司	securities 有价证券
income gain 股利收入	issue 发行
opening price 开盘	closing price 收盘
hard time 低潮	break 暴跌
bond/debenture 债券	Wall Street 华尔街
debtor 债务人；借方	borrower 借方；借款人
discount 贴现；折扣	rediscount 再贴现

③ 广告 Advertisements

🔵 高频单句大放送

01. Clever advertisements are just temptations to spend money.
巧妙的广告诱使人花钱。

02. Newspapers, magazines, television and the Internet are important media for advertising.
报纸、杂志、电视和因特网，这些都是重要的广告媒体。

03. We hired an advertising company for help to sell our product.
我们雇用了一家广告公司来推销我们的产品。

04. There is too much advertising gimmickry.
广告花招太多了。

05. They are credulous people who believe in the advertisement.
他们是一些轻信广告的人。

06. There are many insertions of advertisement in the newspapers.
报纸上有很多插入的广告。

07. He is an advertisement writer.
他是一位广告记者。

08. There are so many advertisement boards on the road.
路上有许多广告牌。

09. I receive a lot of advertisement letters every day.
每天我都收到很多广告邮件。

10. Many others think advertisements are very unpleasant.
很多人认为广告很讨厌。

🔵 口语问答面对面

Sophia: Nowadays, more and more advertisements appear on newspapers, broadcasts, magazines as well as streets.

Anna: Yeah, there are so many advertisements.

索菲娅: 现在越来越多的广告出现在报纸、广播、杂志甚至街头。

安娜: 是啊, 广告太多了。

Sophia: What's your opinion on advertisements?

Anna: As for me, I think advertisements are very unpleasant. I think people are often cheated by the false advertisement on which people always waste a great deal of time.

索菲娅: 你对广告有什么看法?

安娜: 对于我来说, 我觉得广告很令人讨厌。消费者经常被虚假广告欺骗, 而且人们在这些广告上浪费了大量的时间。

Anna: We can't believe everything that is from the advertisement.

Sophia: Absolutely.

安娜: 我们不能完全相信广告。

索菲娅: 当然。

Anna: What's more, I feel annoyed to be interrupted when I am watching TV plays.

Sophia: So advertisements should be limited, I think.

安娜: 更有甚者, 我觉得看电视剧时插播广告特让人心烦。

索菲娅: 因此, 我觉得广告应该受到限制。

Anna: But whether you like it or not, advertisements have become a part of our life.

Sophia: We cannot help but accept it.

安娜: 但是不管你喜不喜欢广告，它已经成为我们生活的一部分。

索菲娅: 我们不得不接受啊。

Anna: How much do we need to pay for such advertising?

Sophia: Well, it depends.

安娜: 做这些广告需要多少费用？

索菲娅: 呃，这得看情况了。

Anna: Can you use your advertising to drum up some business?

Sophia: Yes.

安娜: 能否凭借你的广告来促进一下业务？

索菲娅: 可以。

Anna: What do you mean?

Sophia: It is effective at building awareness, knowledge and a long-term image for the product.

安娜: 你的意思是？

索菲娅: 在为产品创造知名度、增进对产品的了解和建立长期的形象方面，广告是很有效的。

Anna: We should make different commercials for each age group.

Sophia: Yeah. That's reasonable.

安娜: 我们应该针对不同的年龄人群制作不同的广告。

索菲娅: 嗯，有道理。

Anna: I think we should go to an advertising agency.

Sophia: Why?

安娜: 我认为我们得找个广告代理公司。

索菲娅: 为什么？

🌑 情景单词快记忆

CD (creative director) 创作总监

ACD (associated creative director) 副创作总监

advertising agency 广告代理商

advertising campaign 广告活动

177

account director 客户部经理	advertising department 广告部
media director 媒介总监	airport advertising 机场广告
AD (art director) 美术指导	audio-visual advertising 视听广告
AE (account executive) 客户服务人员	billboard advertising 路牌广告
visualizer 插图家；插画师	brand advertising 品牌广告
studio manager 画房经理	bus stop pillar advertising 站牌广告
finish artist 画师	classified advertising 分类广告
CF (commercial film) 广告影片	community advertising 社区广告
account service 客户服务	

读书笔记

23　市场贸易
Market Trade

① 市场调查 Marketing Research

🔵 高频单句大放送

01. We'll have a market research this month.
这个月我们将进行一次市场调查。

02. The recent marketing research shows that our products have an advantage over the others.
最近的市场调查显示我们的产品比其他的占优势。

03. Our market share has been increasing in the past 10 months.
在过去的十个月中我们的市场份额持续上升。

04. I'm here today to present my research result.
我今天来这是为了呈上我的调查结果。

05. If you'll take a look at this chart, the best media mix would be a combination of TV and magazine advertisements.
如果各位看一下这张图表，就可以知道，最好的媒体组合是电视和杂志广告并用。

06. In order to enlarge our new market, we should make a particular plan.
为了扩大我们的市场，我们要制订一个具体的计划。

07. Can you tell them how to make a questionnaire?
能告诉他们怎么去做问卷调查吗?

08. According to the new survey, the New Concept English has a good market in China.
根据最新调查，新概念英语书在中国有很好的市场。

09. The final data shows that there is a slide in the stock market.
根据最终数据显示，股票市场有所下滑。

10. This kind of detergent is of good quality and has a good market in this area.
这种洗涤剂质量好，并且在这一地区有很好的市场。

● 口语问答面对面

Mike: Do you come to Datong frequently?

John: Well, every time I take a trip around Shanxi, I will drop here.

迈克: 你经常来大同吗?

约翰: 嗯, 每当我到山西来旅游时就会顺便到大同来。

Mike: Then you must be very familiar with the coal markets in that part of the world. Do you mind giving me a rundown on it?

John: My honour.

迈克: 那你一定对该地的煤炭市场相当熟悉了。您介意给我介绍一下吗?

约翰: 很荣幸。

Mike: Can you give me some idea on how the market are going at present?

John: Well, just so-so, I should say, neither too bright nor dark.

迈克: 你是否知道目前的市场状况如何?

约翰: 呃, 马马虎虎。我应该说不很好, 也不很坏。

Mike: How about our products in an domestic market?

John: Price is OK, but in terms of its guaranteed service over a long period of time, I would say no.

迈克: 你认为我们的产品在国内市场上具有足够的竞争力吗?

约翰: 就价格来讲是可以的, 但从保证长期服务的角度来看, 我就要说不行了。

John: I'll keep your words in mind. Well, I appreciate your time and thank you so much.

Mike: That's OK. At your service.

约翰: 我会记住你说的话的。哦, 占用您的时间了, 非常感谢。

迈克: 别客气, 随时欢迎。

John: Do you have any particular plan to open up new markets?

Mike: We have decided to strengthen market research.

约翰: 为了开拓新的市场, 你有何具体计划?

迈克: 我们决定加强市场调研。

John: How about our market share?

Mike: Our market share has fallen in the past 3 months.

约翰: 我们公司的市场占有率怎么样?

迈克: 我们的市场份额在过去的三个月里有所下降。

John: Our recent marketing research shows that we will have a chance to beat our rivals by putting new products on the market.

Mike: That's wonderful.

约翰: 我们近来的研究报告显示，通过把新产品推向市场的方式很有可能打败对手。

迈克: 好极了。

John: Do we need market research?

Mike: Yes, of course.

约翰: 我们需要市场调研吗?

迈克: 当然需要了。

John: Are you responsible for the questionaire design?

Mike: Yes.

约翰: 你负责设计调查问卷吗?

迈克: 是的。

🔵 情景单词快记忆

allocation of funds 资金分配	contribution of funds 资金捐献
working capital fund 周转基金	revolving fund 循环基金; 周转性基金
contingency fund 意外开支, 准备金	reserve fund 准备金
buffer fund 缓冲基金, 平准基金	sinking fund 偿债基金
investor 投资人	self-financing 自筹经费; 经费自给
current account 经常账户	current-account holder 支票账户
cheque 支票 (美作: check)	ready money 现钱
ready money business 现金交易; 概不赊欠	banknote/note 钞票; 纸币
exchange rate 汇率; 兑换率	foreign exchange 外汇
capital flight 资本外逃	securities business 证券市场

② 招标和投标 Tendering & Bidding

🔵 高频单句大放送

01. When will you start to bid?
    你们什么时候投标?

02. Can you introduce more about the conditions for the invitation?

能更详细地给我讲述一下招标条件吗？

03. This time we'll tender publicly.
    这次我们将公开竞标。

04. We'll provide you with the guarantee of a standby L/C which is established by the ICBC.
    我们将向你们提供由中国工商银行开立的备用信用证作担保。

05. We'll do our best to win this award.
    我们将尽全力争取得标。

06. We have gotten the bid ready.
    我们已经准备好报价了。

07. The bidder shall bear all costs associated with the preparation and submission of its bid.
    投标人须承担由编制和提交其投标书产生的一切费用。

08. We agree to abide by the conditions of tender specified above.
    我们同意遵守以上规定的投标条款。

09. Did you hear the tender notice?
    你听到招标通知了吗？

10. Do you know the date of the closing of tender?
    你知道招标的截止日期吗？

口语问答面对面

A: This is our Submission of Tender which includes the information about volume of the project, the cost and so on.
B: OK! We'll see it.
A: 这是我们公司的投标书，包括工程量、项目费用等。
B: 好的。我们知道了。

A: What kind of guarantee are you going to provide for us?
B: We can provide you with standby letter of credit established by Bank of China.
A: 贵公司向我们提供什么样的担保呢？
B: 我们提供由中国银行开立的备用信用证。

A: Should we pay earnest money?
B: Yes, you are supposed to pay it on time. If you don't furnish a tender bond on time, your tender will not be considered. Besides, you also should provide

detailed engineering of the goods.

A: 我们要交担保金吗?

B: 是的。你们应该按时交。如果你们没有按时交纳，那么你们的投标将不被考虑在内。除此之外，你们也应该提供货物的详细设计。

A: Where do we submit the tender?

B: To our office which is on the third floor.

A: 我们在哪儿交投标书?

B: 在三层的办事处。

A: Oh, I see. By the way, is tender opening done publicly?

B: Yes. All the bidders will be invited to join us to supervise the tender opening.

A: 我知道了。顺便问一下这次是公开开标吗?

B: 是的，所有的投标人都参加监视。

A: And are the prices stated in the US dollar?

B: Yes. So far as we know, in the field, your company has lots of experience, and we hope you'll consider the tender seriously.

A: 那么用美元标的价吗?

B: 是的。据我们所知贵公司在这方面很有经验。我们希望你们能认真考虑这次投标。

A: I'm glad to hear that you've decided to take part in the bid. Have you prepared your bid?

B: We have prepared a competitive bid.

A: 我非常高兴听说你们决定参加竞标，你们准备好报价了吗?

B: 我们已经准备好了竞争力强的报价。

A: We're very interested in this tender, and we'll do our best to win this award.

B: We hope so, too.

A: 我们对这次招标非常感兴趣，我们一定尽全力争取得标。

B: 我们也希望如此。

A: When do you start the invitation?

B: Next month.

A: 你们什么时候招标?

B: 下个月。

A: Would you please let me know more about your conditions for the tender?

B: Invitation will be sent next week. And you could find the details.

A: 能否请您把招标条件更详细地向我介绍一下?

B: 下周我们就发出招标通知。详情您一看就明白了。

情景单词快记忆

bidding 招标	bid 投标 (投标文件)
bidder 投标人	tenderee 招标人
bid inviting party 招标方	invitation for bids 投标邀请
instructions to bidders 投标人须知	eligible bidders 合格的投标人
bidding documents 招标文件	bid prices 投标价格
tendering company 招标公司	original bid 投标文件正本
copy of bid 投标文件副本	bid security 投标保证金
bid opening 开标	tender notice 招标通知
date of the closing of tender 招标截止日期	general conditions of tender 招标条件
Invitation to Bid 投标邀请书	submission of tenders 投标
tender documents 投标文件	Bid Bond 投标押金；押标金
evaluation of bids 投标评估	work out tender documents 做标；编标

③ 银行业务 Bank Service

高频单句大放送

01. Can you change some money, please?
能否请你给我兑换一些钱?

02. Would you kindly sign the exchange form, giving your name and address?
请在兑换单上签字，写上你的姓名和地址好吗?

03. I'd like to know if you could change this money back into U.S. dollars for me.
我想知道能否把这笔兑回成美元。

04. Could you give me some small notes?
给我一些小票好吗?

05. We hand you our account on the bar iron, amounting to $512,000, which kindly pass to our credit.
兹奉上以我方为贷方的棒铁总价为 512,000 美元清单一份。

06. You should provide some supporting materials for opening an export L/C.
你需要为开立出口信用证提供一些相关的证明。

07. Please fill out an application form.
请填写一份申请表。

08. Generally speaking, commercial banks account for most of international trading financing.
一般来说，商业银行负责大多数的国际贸易融资。

09. How much do you want to honor it in case?
你打算兑付多少现金呢?

10. I need 300 dollars in 100-dollar cheques.
我要 300 美元票面为 100 美元的支票。

口语问答面对面

Customer: Good morning, sir. I am from Japan. My English is poor. Can you help me?

Clerk: It is my pleasure, but I think it would be better for you to tell me what you want to do.

顾客: 你好，先生。我是日本人。我的英语不太好，你能帮忙吗?

职员: 很高兴为您效劳，但我想您最好告诉我您想要干什么。

Customer: Oh, I want to change some money, but I do not know how to fill out the exchange memo.

Clerk: Would you care to give me your passport and write your name on the paper?

顾客: 啊，我想兑换些钱，但不知道怎样填写兑换水单。

职员: 您能把您的护照给我，并把您的名字写在这张纸上吗?

Clerk: Good. I will fill out the exchange memo for you now. Why do not you take a seat over there for a moment?

Customer: I would like to. Thanks.

职员: 好，我现在就为您填写这张兑换水单。您请在那里坐一会行吗?

顾客: 好的，谢谢。

Clerk: Hello, Mr. Tanaka. I was wondering if you would ever thought of conversing the unused Renminbi back into Japan Yen later?

Customer: Yes, if I have Renminbi left.

职员: 您好，田中先生，不知道您是否考虑到以后要把没有用完的人民币兑换成日元呢?
顾客: 是的，如果有没用完的人民币的话，就要换成日元。

Clerk: If I may make a suggestion, please keep your exchange memo safe.
Customer: Thank you indeed. I will do that.
职员: 那么，如果我还可以提一个建议的话，请您保管好您的这张兑换水单。
顾客: 我会保管好的。谢谢。

Customer: I want to cash the draft.
Clerk: Yes. You can have your collected draft paid by submitting the collecting documents.
顾客: 我想兑付汇票。
职员: 好的。你可凭有关拖收文件兑付您的汇票。

Clerk: How would you like to withdraw the amount?
Customer: I'd like to have some cash. Then perhaps I'll have the rest by check.
职员: 你打算怎么提取这些款项呢?
顾客: 我想要一部分现金，剩下的那部分可能就开成支票。

Clerk: How much would you like to honor it in cash?
Customer: 500 US dollars in cash, the other 500 US dollars in a check.
职员: 你想兑付多少现金?
顾客: 兑付500美元现金并将它们兑换成人民币，其余的500美元兑换成支票。

A: The bank's export financing is really important for our company.
B: Why is it?
A: 银行的出口卖方信贷对我们公司来说很重要。
B: 为什么?

A: What does commercial bank account for?
B: Commercial banks account for most of international trading financing.
A: 商业银行负责什么?
B: 商业银行负责大多数的国际贸易融资。

🔵 情景单词快记忆

National City Bank of New York 花旗银行	People's Bank of China 中国人民银行
American Oriental Banking Corporation 美丰银行	Bank of China 中国银行

The Chase Bank 大通银行	Construction Bank 建设银行
European Investment Bank (EIB) 欧洲投资银行	Industrial and Commercial Bank 工商银行
Midland Bank Ltd. 米兰银行	central bank 中央银行
United Bank of Switzerland 瑞士联合银行	investment bank 投资银行
Bank of Tokyo Ltd. 东京银行	local bank 本地银行
Hongkong and Shanghai Corporation 香港汇丰银行	domestic bank 国内银行
Food and Agricultural Organization (FAO) 粮食与农业组织；粮农组织	paying bank 付款银行
World Bank 世界银行	trust bank 信托银行

读书笔记

24 商务出行
Business Travel

① 商务出行 Business Trip

高频单句大放送

01. Can you tell me your departure date?
能告诉我您的出发日期吗？

02. Would you like me to book a room for you in the hotel?
需要我为您预订酒店房间吗？

03. I want to reserve a seat from Los Angeles to Tokyo.
我要预订一张从洛杉矶到东京的机票。

04. I want a package deal including airfare and hotel.
我需要一个成套服务，包括机票和住宿。

05. I'd like to reserve a sleeper to Chicago.
我要预订去芝加哥的卧铺。

06. Would you like to take the first class as usual?
您还是和往常一样坐头等舱吗？

07. The company will reimburse everything.
公司会报销所有费用。

08. I have nothing to declare.
我没申报的东西。

09. It's all personal effects.
这些东西都是私人用品。

10. The flight number is AK708 on September 5th.
这趟航班是 9 月 5 号的 AK708。

口语问答面对面

Jean: Guess what! The boss is sending me to the West Coast for a marketing seminar next month.

Chandler: Ah hah, you must be happy. You've been itching to go on a business trip for months.

简: 你猜怎么着! 老板下个月要我去西海岸参加一个市场营销研讨会。

钱德勒: 啊哈，你肯定很高兴。你想出差都想好几个月了。

Jean: Will I use the card for everything?

Chandler: No, we have company credit arrangements with some major airlines and hotels. For this trip, you'll probably only use it for food. Not all restaurants accept the card, so you may have to pay cash.

简: 一切费用都要用那张卡吗?

钱德勒: 不，我们和一些主要航空公司和酒店都有公司信用协议。这次旅行你也许只会用它来吃饭。但并不是所有的饭店都接受这种信用卡。你也许要付现金。

Jean: Anything else?

Chandler: Since you'll be travelling often, apply for a frequent flyer card. Gathering frequent flyer miles is one of the perks of OCS travel. And let me know how you like living out of a suitcase.

简: 还有其他的吗?

钱德勒: 既然你要经常出差，去申请一张飞行积分卡。积累飞行里程是商务旅行的额外补助之一。到时候告诉我你是怎么带着旅行包生活的。

Jean: When do you plan to leave?

Chandler: Next Monday.

简: 您打算什么时候走?

钱德勒: 下周一。

Jean: How would you like to go?

Chandler: By plane.

简: 您打算乘什么交通工具?

钱德勒: 乘飞机。

Jean: Will the company reimburse everything?

Chandler: Of course, it will.

简: 公司会报销所有费用吗?

钱德勒: 当然。

Jean: What about travelers' cheques and foreign currency?

Chandler: The usual amounts.

简: 您带多少旅行支票和外币?

钱德勒: 和往常一样。

Jean: What can I do for you?

Chandler: I need to know what the weather there will be like.

简: 需要什么帮助吗?

钱德勒: 我需要知道当地的气候。

Jean: Have you found all the necessary documents?

Chandler: Yes, I've got them all prepared.

简: 您找到所有必需的文件了吗?

钱德勒: 是的，都准备好了。

Jean: I'll send you the schedule as soon as possible.

Chandler: Thank you so much.

简: 我会尽快把旅行时间表给您送去。

钱德勒: 谢谢。

情景单词快记忆

John F Kennedy International Airport 肯尼迪机场	Jandakot Airport 詹达科特机场
Gatwick Airport 盖特威克机场	Perth International Airport 珀斯国际机场
Heathrow Airport 希思罗机场	Metropolitan Area Airport 都市区机场
Waterloo Airport 滑铁卢机场	Seattle-Tacoma International Airport 西雅图塔科马国际机场
Luton Airport 卢顿机场	Liverpool John Lennon Airport 利物浦约翰列侬机场
Stansted Airport 斯坦斯特机场	economy room (ER) 经济间
London City Airport 伦敦城市机场	standard room (SR) 标准间
Sydney Bankstown Airport 悉尼班克斯镇机场	superior room (UR) 高级套房
Sydney Water Airport 悉尼水利局机场	deluxe room (DR) 豪华间
Kingsford Smith Airport 金斯福德史密斯机场	presidential suit (PS) 总统套房
Sydney West Airport 悉尼西机场	

② 买票 Buying the Ticket

🔵 高频单句大放送

01. Can I help you?
    需要帮忙吗?

02. I want to buy two single-way tickets to Shanghai, please.
    我要买两张去上海的单程车票。

03. I want two return tickets to Suzhou, please.
    请买两张去苏州的回程票。

04. For when?
    几点的?

05. How do you want to fly: coach or first class?
    您想要什么:经济舱还是头等舱?

06. I want the tourist class.
    我要经济舱的。

07. Here's your ticket, sir. It's all in order.
    先生,这是您的机票。全部办妥了。

08. May I have your name and flight number, please?
    请问您的姓名和班机号?

09. If you excuse me for a second. I'll find out for you.
    请稍候片刻。我给您检查一下。

10. How long will the journey take?
    全程得花多少时间?

🔵 口语问答面对面

A: Good morning. The United Airlines, what can I do for you?
B: Yes, I'd like to make a reservation to Boston next week.
A: 早上好。美国联合航空公司。我能为您做些什么?
B: 是的,我想订一张下周飞往波士顿的机票。

A: When do you want to fly?
B: Monday, September 12.
A: 您想何时去?
B: 周一,9月12日。

A: We have Flight 802 on monday. Just a moment please. Let me check whether there're seats available. I'm sorry we are all booked up for Flight 802 on that day.

B: Then, any alternatives?

A: 我们有周一 802 次航班。请稍等，让我查一下那天是否有座。非常抱歉 802 次航班机票已订完。

B: 那还有别的吗？

A: The next available flight leaves at 9:30, Tuesday morning, September 13. Shall I book you a seat?

B: It is a direct flight, isn't it?

A: 下一趟航班在 9 月 13 日周二上午 9:30 起飞。我能为您订个座位吗？

B: 是直航对吗？

A: You want to go first class or coach?

B: I prefer first class.

A: 您愿意订头等舱还是经济舱的机票？

B: 我想订头等舱的机票。

A: What is the fare?

B: One way is $176.

A: 多少钱？

B: 单程是 176 美元。

B: OK, I will take the 9:30 flight on Tuesday.

A: A seat on Flight 807 to Boston, at 9:30, Tuesday morning.

B: 好的，我将订周二 9:30 的机票。

A: 一张 807 次航班周二早晨 9:30 飞往波士顿的机票。

A: Is it all right, sir?

B: Right.

A: 对吗，先生？

B: 对。

A: Can you also put me on the waiting list for the 12th?

B: Certainly.

A: 你能把我放到 12 号等候名单中吗？

B: 当然可以。

A: May I have your name & telephone number?

B: My name is Lorus Anderson. You can reach me at 52378651.

A: 请您告诉我您的名字和联系方式？

B: 我叫洛里斯·安德森。拨打 52378651 您能和我联系。

A: I will notify you if there is cancellation.

B: Thank you very much.

A: 若有取消我将通知您。

B: 非常感谢。

🔵 情景单词快记忆

book the ticket/make a reservation 火车票 / 飞机票预订	(ticket) scalper 黄牛；票贩子
all booked up/full booked 订满了	cancel/cancellation 取消订票
direct flight 直航	local train 慢车
direct train 直达列车	special express 特快
hard seat 硬座	soft seat 软座
semi cushioned berth 硬卧	cushioned berth 软卧
sleeping berth/sleeper (of train) 卧铺	(train) ticket for standing room 站票
temporary train 临客列车	bullet train 动车
speculative reselling of tickets/ticket scalping 倒票	high-speed train 高铁
train attendant 乘务员	trial operation 试运行
real-name purchasing system 实名制购票	luxury train seat 豪华座
business class 商务座	standard seat 普通座
purified water 纯净水	

③ 酒店入住 Check-in

🔵 高频单句大放送

01. How much is the room, please?
    请问房价是多少？

02. Is hot water available any time?
    任何时间都有热水吗？

03. How long do you intend to stay?
    您打算住多久？

04. Do you have a single room?
    你们有单人间吗？

05. I'm staying at least a week.
    我至少将住一周。

06. Where can I check in?
    在哪儿办理登记手续？

07. I'd like to check into a room in your hotel.
    我想要间客房。

08. I'd like to check-in, please.
    我要登记住宿。

09. My friend booked a room for me.
    我朋友替我订了一间房。

10. Do you have any rooms available?
    你们还有空房间吗？

🔵 口语问答面对面

Clerk: Hi. Good afternoon. What can I do for you?
Anne: I have a reservation.
职员: 嗨! 下午好，我能为您效劳吗?
安妮: 我有预订。

Clerk: May I ask your name?
Anne: Anne Smith.
职员: 请问您的名字?
安妮: 安妮·史密斯。

Anne: Is it all right?
Clerk: Yes.
安妮: 这样可以吗?
职员: 可以。

Clerk: Will you be paying by cash or credit card?
Anne: Cash.
职员: 你要付现金还是用信用卡?
安妮: 付现金。

Clerk: In that case, we will need a one-night's deposit. That'll be eighty dollars.

Anne: OK. Here you are.

职员: 这样，我们要收取一晚的保证金，80美元。

安妮: 好，给你。

Clerk: Here's your receipt and your key.

Anne: Thank you. And I'd like a wake-up call at 7 o'clock tomorrow morning.

职员: 这是您的收据和钥匙。

安妮: 谢谢。我想请你们在明天早上7点打电话叫醒我。

Clerk: Just call the hotel operator to arrange for a wake-up call.

Anne: OK.

职员: 请打给旅馆接线生安排早叫电话。

安妮: 好的。

Anne: By the way, can I mail items from the hotel?

Clerk: Yes, we have mail service. You can call the business service center. They know the ropes.

安妮: 另外，我能从酒店邮寄东西吗？

职员: 可以，我们有邮寄服务。您可以拨打商务服务中心电话。他们精通这项业务。

Clerk: May I have the receipt?

Anne: Of course, here you are.

职员: 可以给我收据吗？

安妮: 当然可以，给您。

Anne: When will be your checking out time?

Clerk: Before 1:00 P.M.

安妮: 你们的退房时间是几点？

职员: 下午一点前。

情景单词快记忆

hotel 旅馆	guest house 宾馆
main entrance 大门	entrance hall 门厅
staircase/stairs/stairway 楼梯	balustrade/banister 楼梯栏杆
corridor 过道	veranda 外廊

lobby 走廊	lift/elevator 电梯
information desk 问询处	reception office 接待室
hotel register 旅客登记簿	registration form 登记表
newsstand 售报处	postal service 邮局服务处
shop 小卖部	bar 酒吧间
lounge 休息厅	roof garden 屋顶花园

读书笔记

第三章

娱乐休闲英语

25 文化漫谈 Culture

① 星座 Constellation

高频单句大放送

01. What's your sign?
你是什么星座的？

02. Sagittarius is fire energy. This is a very active, extroverted sign.
射手座是火象星座。这个星座非常主动、外向。

03. Scorpio is a water element, and this makes it a somewhat enigmatic sign.
水象星座的特质使天蝎座有些神秘。

04. Leo is fire to the core.
狮子座是火象星座的中心。

05. The Earth element of Taurus brings strength and the desire for solid ground form and structure.
土象星座的特质让金牛座渴望并具有脚踏实地的能力。

06. Good memory is Cancer's born gift.
良好的记忆力是巨蟹座与生俱来的天赋。

07. Libra is a sign that is more extroverted and active.
天秤座的特性比较外向和主动。

08. Patience and caution are Capricorn's advantages.
摩羯座的优点是坚持不懈和谨慎。

09. Diligence is Virgo's advantage.
处女座的优点是勤奋。

10. Virgo actually find, the encyclopedia exciting and reads self-help and fitness books for fun.
处女座可能会觉得百科全书、自助书籍或健身书籍很有趣。

口语问答面对面

Lily: What's the trouble with you?
Pat: I wonder what gift I should give my girlfriend.

丽莉: 你怎么了?

帕特: 我在发愁给我女朋友买什么礼物。

Lily: Oh, what's her sign? Maybe I can give you some suggestions.

Pat: Really? She is a Leo.

丽莉: 噢, 她是什么星座的? 或许我可以给你一些意见。

帕特: 真的吗? 她是狮子座的。

Lily: Let me check it for you. It is said that Leo is easy to shop for if you can carry much gold. Gifts of gold are the things for Leo. Anything classy and monogrammed will usually work. Theater tickets to the best play will also go over big. Then I think you can give her a ticket for her.

Pat: Great. Then I will see what's on at the moment.

丽莉: 我帮你查一查。上面说狮子座的人比较容易买礼物,如果你有那么多金钱的话。金子做的礼物就是送给狮子座的东西。任何亮丽而有花纹图案的东西一般都能行得通。好戏剧的戏票也很受欢迎。我想你可以送她一张戏票。

帕特: 太好了! 那我去看看这几天有什么在上映的电影。

Lily: What's your sign?

Pat: Well, I'm an Aries. So what?

丽莉: 你是什么星座啊?

帕特: 嗯, 我是白羊座。怎么了?

Lily: From your signs, I can tell you how your relations with your girlfriend.

Pat: Oh, I see.

丽莉: 从你们的星座, 我就可以告诉你你们的关系会怎么样。

帕特: 噢, 我明白了。

Lily: Great! You are good and having a lasting relationship.

Pat: I'd like to hear that.

丽莉: 很棒啊! 你们是个甜蜜持久的组合。

帕特: 这句话我爱听。

Lily: What's your sign?

Pat: I'm a Libra.

丽莉: 你是什么星座?

帕特: 我是天秤座。

Lily: No wonder you're so sociable.

Pat: What's your sign then?

丽莉: 难怪你擅长交际。

帕特: 那你是什么星座呢?

Pat: What's your boyfriend's sign?

Lily: He is an Sagittarius.

帕特: 你男朋友是什么星座呢?

丽莉: 他是射手座的。

情景单词快记忆

Ecliptic 黄道	Gemini 双子座
Leo 狮子座	Lepus 天兔座
Libra 天秤座	Milky way 银河
Monoceros 麒麟座	Pisces 双鱼座
Polaris/polestar 北极星	Pollux 北河三
Procyon 南河三	Scorpio/Scorpius 天蝎座
Scutum 盾牌座	Sirius/Dog Star 天狼星
summer solstice 夏至点	Taurus 金牛座
Triangulum 三角座	Tropic of Cancer 北回归线
Tucana 杜鹃座	Vega 织女星
vernal equinoctial point 春分点	Virgo 处女座
Altair 牵牛星	Andromeda 仙女座
Aries 白羊座	autumnal equinoctial point 秋分点
Big Dipper 北斗七星	Cancer 巨蟹座
Canes Venatici 猎犬座	Capricornus 摩羯座

② 读书看报 Reading

高频单句大放送

01. What's the current best-seller?

当今最畅销的书是什么?

02. Is there a newsstand near here?

这儿有报亭吗?

03. Excuse me, where can I find children's books?
请问儿童书籍在哪里？

04. What are you reading recently?
你最近在读什么？

05. I could hardly open a book these days.
这些日子以来我很少看书。

06. What's your favorite magazine?
你最喜欢的杂志是什么？

07. I'd like to buy *Harry Potter* by J·K Rowling.
我想要买 J.K. 罗琳所写的《哈利·波特》。

08. What's your favorite part of this book?
你最喜欢这本书的哪一个部分？

09. I'm at the very end of the book.
我快要看完这本书了。

10. I have no idea what to read. Please give me a recommended reading list.
我不知道要看些什么书。请给我一份推荐书单。

口语问答面对面

George: Good morning, Brian. Have you finished reading the novel you bought last week?
Brian: No, I was very busy yesterday. I only finished reading half of it.
乔治: 早上好，布莱恩。你看完上周买的那本小说了吗？
布莱恩: 还没有，我昨天特别忙。我只读了一半。

George: When will you plan to finish reading it?
Brian: About three days more, I think.
乔治: 你打算什么时候读完这本小说？
布莱恩: 我想大约还要三天时间。

George: Well, I'll come to you for it three days later.
Brian: No problem.
乔治: 那么，三天后我去取。
布莱恩: 没问题。

George: Do you think this novel is interesting?
Brian: Yes, it is. But there are many characters in it, and sometimes you'll be confused.

乔治: 你认为这本小说有趣吗?
布莱恩: 是的, 很有趣。但里面有很多人物, 有时会把你弄糊涂的。

Brian: And there is a saying, "It's never too late to learn." Reading is a good way to learn.
George: You are quite right. I wish I had more time for reading.
布莱恩: 常言道"活到老, 学到老"。读书是很好的学习方式。
乔治: 你说得对。我希望有更多的时间来看书。

Brian: Doesn't that take up a lot of your time?
George: Well, no, because I only read those sections that interest me.
布莱恩: 看那个要花很多时间吗?
乔治: 不用很多时间, 因为我只看那些我感兴趣的部分。

Brian: Is this novel interesting?
George: Yes, it is.
布莱恩: 这部小说有意思吗?
乔治: 是的, 很有意思。

Brian: What kind of books do you like to read?
George: I like reading romance.
布莱恩: 你喜欢读哪种书?
乔治: 我喜欢读浪漫小说。

Brian: What's your favorite book?
George: It's a little hard to say. I think maybe *Jane Eyre* is my favorite.
布莱恩: 你最喜欢的是哪本书?
乔治: 很难说, 我想《简·爱》是我最喜欢的一本。

Brian: Which section are you looking at?
George: The sports section. It's very interesting.
布莱恩: 你看的是哪一部分?
乔治: 是体育部分, 很有趣。

情景单词快记忆

anecdote 轶闻趣事	around nation 国内新闻版
around the world 国际新闻版	Associated Press（AP）美联社

banner headline 头号大标题	blurb 商品信息
book review 书评	bookworm 书虫；书呆子
briefing 简报	brief 简讯
budget 要闻索引	circulation 发行量
city news 社会新闻	comics 连环漫画
communique 公报	cover story 封面报道
creator 创造者	critique 评论
culture and sports 文化与体育栏	economics and business 经贸版
editorial 社论	entertainment 娱乐版
entire 全部的	exclusive news 独家新闻
fabricate 捏造；杜撰	financial section 金融版
front-page news 头版新闻	

3 谈论他人 Talking About Others

高频单句大放送

01. Although she's beautiful in appearance, she's too ugly in her heart.
尽管她外表美丽，但内心十分丑陋。

02. Her sister is very plump.
她的姐姐非常丰满。

03. His grandfather is advanced in age.
他的爷爷年事已高。

04. What's the weight of your daughter?
你女儿体重是多少？

05. What's his girlfriend's height?
他女朋友有多高？

06. Sally is not twenty-four yet.
萨利还不到 24 岁。

07. So slender the girl is!
那个女孩真苗条！

08. The little boy's nose is flat.
这个小男孩的鼻子是扁平的。

09. He's a fine-looking man while his wife is plain.
他很英俊然而他的妻子却相貌平平。

10. Tina has a short temper, so nobody likes her.
    蒂娜脾气不好，所以没有人喜欢她。

🌐 口语问答面对面

Bailey: Hi, Cailyn. Who's the girl together with you yesterday?
Cailyn: She's my sister. And she's two years older than me.
贝莉: 嗨，凯琳。昨天和你一起的那个女孩子是谁啊?
凯琳: 她是我姐姐。比我大两岁。

Bailey: Wow, she's so beautiful! Is she still a student?
Cailyn: Thank you! Yes, she is, and you know she's the beauty of her university.
贝莉: 哇，她真漂亮啊! 她还是个学生吧?
凯琳: 谢谢! 是的，她是，并且她还是她们大学校花呢。

Bailey: Can you tell me something more about her?
Cailyn: Yes, of course. She's a plain, ambitious and very kind girl. And she gets
        the scholarship every year. Since she attended the university she'd never
        asked her parents for money.
贝莉: 你能告诉我更多关于她的事情吗?
凯琳: 是的，当然。她是一个朴素、有上进心和善良的女孩子。每年都能拿到奖学金。
      自从她上了大学就再也没有向爸妈要钱了。

Bailey: Oh, so excellent she is! I'm very jealous of her.
Cailyn: Yes, I also want to be the one like her.
贝莉: 哦，她真的很优秀! 很羡慕她啊。
凯琳: 是啊，我也想成为像她那样的。

Bailey: I guess there must be many boys going for her. Does she have a
        boyfriend now?
Cailyn: Yes, you're right. But she still hasn't had a boyfriend yet.
贝莉: 我猜一定有很多男孩子追求她吧。她现在有男朋友了吗?
凯琳: 是的。但是她仍然没有男朋友。

Bailey: She must have a high standard for her boyfriend.
Cailyn: Not really. She always pays little attention to find a boyfriend. She says
        she wants to spend most of time on her study.
贝莉: 她挑选男朋友的标准一定很高。

凯琳: 不是这样的。她从来都很少关注找男友的事情。她说她想把大部分时间花在学习上。

Bailey: She is a dedicated fan of tomboys.

Cailyn: But I think she has a boyish charm.

贝莉: 她是中性美女的忠实粉丝。

凯琳: 但是我觉得她有一种像男孩子一样的魅力。

Bailey: Stop trying to act toughly. This isn't the right time. You've got to learn how to use your girlish charms.

Cailyn: Don't worry about it. It's alright to be a tomboy.

贝莉: 不要男孩子气了，这可不是时候，你一定要学会怎样运用你的女人魅力。

凯琳: 别担心，做一个假小子也没什么的。

Bailey: I have such a big crush on that tomboy girl in class.

Cailyn: I think we all do!

贝莉: 我疯狂地爱上了班里的那个假小子。

凯琳: 我想我们都是!

Bailey: His daughter is a saucy tomboy.

Cailyn: Yeah, she has always been a tomboy. She likes hiking and horseback riding.

贝莉: 他的女儿是个调皮的假小子。

凯琳: 是啊，她一直都是个假小子，她喜欢远足和骑马。

情景单词快记忆

timid 胆小的	childish 幼稚的
emotional 情绪化的	lovely 可爱的
humorous 幽默的	naughty 顽皮的
smart 聪明的	brave 勇敢的
warm-hearted 热心的	friendly 友好的
frank 坦率的	gentle 温和的
polite 礼貌的	diligent 勤勉的
rude 粗鲁的	cruel 残酷的
lazy 懒惰的	stupid 愚蠢的

26 玩转时尚 Fashion

① 服装时尚 Clothes and Fashion

高频单句大放送

01. Do you think I look fashionable in this blue dress?
我穿这件蓝裙子看起来是不是很时尚？

02. Is it a name brand?
是名牌的吧？

03. What material is it made from?
这是什么料子的？

04. Do you like the pattern?
你喜欢这种图案吗？

05. That blouse is just not my cup of tea.
那件衬衫实在不是我的风格。

06. They're cute, but not very practical.
很好看，但是不怎么实用。

07. This is my favorite brand of jeans.
我最喜欢这个牌子的牛仔裤。

08. It's too old-fashioned!
太过时了！

09. You don't want to be left out, do you?
你不想落后，是不是？

10. This is the latest style.
这是最新款式。

口语问答面对面

A: What color do you like?
B: I like blue best.
A: 你喜欢什么颜色？
B: 我最喜欢蓝色的。

A: The clothes here are so expensive! No wonder there are few people.

B: Beauty costs, dear! What do you think of this dress? Do you think it suits me?

A: 这儿的衣服真贵！难怪没什么人！

B: 亲爱的，美丽是要付出代价的。你觉得这条裙子怎么样，适合我吗？

A: It's lovely, but to be frank, it's not the most practical. You don't have many formal events in your calendar, do you?

B: Come on, you sound like my mom. Look at it, it's beautiful.

A: 很好看，但是说实话，不太实用。你最近又不用出席什么正式场合，对吧？

B: 拜托，怎么口气跟我妈妈一样！你看看，多漂亮啊！

A: When you buy clothes, you must think about the materials, quality and price.

B: Maybe you have a point.

A: 买衣服的时候，要同时考虑料子、品质和价格。

B: 也许你说得对。

A: Hey, look, that's the same shirt Britney wore in her concert.

B: Exactly! Oh, my god! I love Britney! I'm going to get it.

A: 嘿，你看，那是布兰妮在演唱会上穿过的衬衫！

B: 真的是！天哪！我爱死布兰妮了！我要买下来。

A: Why not try it on?

B: It's just the right size—a perfect fit! I'll take it.

A: 试试吧。

B: 大小正好，太合身了！我买了。

A: It's getting cold.

B: Yes. I bought a scarf yesterday. It's really nice and warm. Have a look.

A: 天气越来越冷了。

B: 是啊。我昨天买了条新围巾，又好看又暖和，你来看看。

A: How does it look on me?

B: It looks great, but you need something to go with it. It's too plain on its own.

A: 好看吗？

B: 很好看，就是你得跟衣服配，不然单独一条围巾太普通了。

A: How about this blue sweater?

B: That's a good idea. When did you buy it? Is it a name brand?

A: 这件蓝色毛衣怎样?
B: 不错。这件毛衣什么时候买的啊，是名牌的吧?

A: That looks lovely. Just one more thing—you need a pair of earrings.
B: I've got a pair of pearl earrings. Here it is.
A: 漂亮极了! 就缺一样东西——耳环。
B: 我有一对珍珠耳环，试试看。

🔵 情景单词快记忆

brand 牌子	broad 宽的
design 设计；图案	detachable 可分开的
discount 折扣	fashion 时髦；流行
good-looking 好看的	leather pants 皮裤
out of date 过时	pattern 图案；样式
style 款式	tight 紧的
wide-legged pants 宽管长裤	wrinkle 起皱纹
gift bag 礼物袋	gift box 礼物盒
gift wrap 礼品包装	gift-wrap 以缎带包装
bow 蝴蝶结	card 卡片；名片

② 选秀节目 Talent Show

🔵 高频单句大放送

01. He got booted after his first audition, but he did not give up.
   海选时刚出场表演他就被淘汰了，但他并没有放弃。

02. He had barely survived the audition and finally got a chance to advance in the contest.
   海选时，他险些淘汰，但最终赢得晋级的机会。

03. In the audition, he has won popularity among the audience.
   海选过程中，他的人气大增。

04. I just fear that my favorite contestant might be knocked out.
   我担心最喜欢的选手会被淘汰。

05. Who knows which candidate will make it to the final?
   谁知道最后哪位选手会得冠军?

06. He really did a great job in the finale, especially in the PK round.
他决赛的表现真好，尤其是在 PK 那一轮。

07. The majority of the audience cast their votes for him.
大多数观众都给他投了票。

08. The host announced that he won it all.
主持人宣布他获得冠军。

09. Have you watched any of the talent shows on TV?
你看过电视上的选秀节目吗？

10. He not only sings well but shows perseverance when he encounters difficulties in the contest.
他不仅歌唱得好，比赛中遇到困难还不屈不挠。

口语问答面对面

A: Did you watch the finale last night? My favorite singer won!

B: Oh, I love him too. He not only sings well but shows perseverance when he encounters difficulties in the contest.

A: 昨天晚上你看决赛了吗？我最喜欢的歌手取得了最后的胜利。

B: 我也很喜欢他。他不仅歌唱得好，比赛中遇到困难还不屈不挠。

A: He got booted after his initial performance in the audition, but he did not give up. He then tried at another two audition.

B: He had barely survived the third audition and finally got a chance to advance in the contest. Fortunately, in the third audition, he has won popularity among the audition. And that's when I started to notice him.

A: 第一次海选时他被淘汰了，但他并没有放弃。之后他又参加了两次海选。

B: 第三次海选时，他险些淘汰，但最终赢得晋级的机会。幸好，第三次海选过程中，他人气大增。我就是那时候开始注意他的。

A: Before he made the top three, I was so nervous. I just fear that he might be knocked out.

B: Yeah, there're so many excellent candidates out there. Who knows which one will make it to the final?

A: 他进入前三名之前我很紧张，怕他被淘汰。

B: 是啊，比赛中有那么多优秀的选手。谁知道最后谁会拿冠军。

A: He really did a great job in the finale, especially in the PK round. He performed so well that the majority of the audience cast their votes for him.

B: And the host announced that he won it all!

A: 他决赛的表现真的很好，尤其是 PK 那一轮，很多观众都因此投票给他。

B: 然后主持人宣布，他最终获得冠军！

A: Have you watched any of the talent shows on TV?

B: Yes, I've watched the finale for the "Super Girl."

A: 你看过电视上的选秀节目吗?

B: 看过，我看过超级女声的决赛。

A: The producer is very smart to copy the program from the US, which is quite fresh and eye-catching for mainland audiences.

B: Yeah, and they know exactly what the audiences have in mind.

A: 制作人真聪明，模仿美国这种新鲜的节目形式，很吸引观众。

B: 是啊，他们知道观众心里想的是什么。

A: Everyone desires "equal opportunities" and a channel to climb up the social ladder all the way to the highest in society.

B: That's why the program has attracted so many star-wannabe.

A: 每个人都想拥有"平等的机会"想爬到社会顶层。

B: 所以这类节目吸引了很多梦想当明星的人。

A: It seems that these talent shows are getting less popular these days. There's no such program this year.

B: Yeah, these programs are gradually losing their appeal.

A: 最近这些选秀节目好像没那么红了。今年就没播这些节目了。

B: 对，人们对这些节目渐渐失去了兴趣。

A: He usually stepped out of line. So will you attend a beauty contest?

B: Impossible! I know I am not made for that.

A: 他真有点儿过分了。那你会参加选美大赛吗?

B: 绝对不可能！我根本就不是那块料。

A: How?

B: He said I was not qualified for a beauty contest.

A: 他怎么挑衅你的?

B: 他说我没资格参加选美大赛。

情景单词快记忆

talent shows 选秀	attend 参加
qualified 有资格的	appeal 兴趣
finale 决赛	attract 吸引
star-wannabe 想当明星的人	audience 观众
initial audition 海选	national final 全国总决赛
beauty contest 选美大赛	announce 宣布

③ 运动健身 Exercise and Fitness

高频单句大放送

01. I'm starting to lose weight since I started going to the gym!
自从我开始去健身房后，我的体重减轻了。

02. How much does a gym membership cost?
成为健身房会员需要多少钱？

03. I want to sign up for a gym membership.
我想报名成为健身房的会员。

04. I need to go to the gym more.
我需要多去几次健身房。

05. Do you have to pay a membership fee?
你要付会员费吗？

06. I went to the health club to work out. All my muscles are sore.
我去健身俱乐部锻炼去了，全身肌肉酸痛。

07. I need a personal trainer.
我需要一个私人教练。

08. Wow, that was a great workout.
哇，健身效果真好！

09. Do you know where the locker room is?
你知道更衣室在哪儿吗？

10. I feel a million bucks after that.
做完运动我感觉好舒畅。

● 口语问答面对面

A: I need to get some more exercise.

B: I'll go with you next time.

A: 我需要做更多的运动。

B: 下次我和你一起去。

A: Do you have to pay a membership fee?

B: Yes, each person has to pay an extra 100 dollars membership fee.

A: 你要交会员费吗?

B: 要交，每个人都需要另缴纳 100 美元的会费。

A: I went to the health club to work out. All my muscles are sore.

B: Did you overdo it with your exercises?

A: 我去健身俱乐部锻炼去了，全身肌肉酸痛。

B: 你运动过量了吧?

A: I'm starting to lose weight since I started going to the gym!

B: That's great to hear. Now if only I could do the same.

A: 自从我开始去健身房后，我的体重减轻了。

B: 听到你这么说真高兴。要是我也一样就好了。

A: I enrolled in a fitness center two months ago.

B: Oh, are you a member in the fitness center?

A: 两个月前我加入了一个健身中心。

B: 哦，你是这个健身中心的会员吗?

A: What are you going to do next?

B: I'm going to spend 30 minutes on the exercise bike.

A: 你接下来要干什么?

B: 我要在骑车器上锻炼 30 分钟。

A: It's too crowded in the gym at weekends.

B: Yeah. But let's warm up first.

A: 周末健身房里太挤了。

B: 是啊，不过咱们还是先热身吧。

A: Why do you think I need a personal trainer?

B: Because a coach can help you reach your fitness goals.

A: 你为什么觉得我需要一个私人教练？
B: 因为教练可以帮你达到健身的目标。

A: No matter how busy I am, I will always squeeze some time for exercise.
B: Oh, what kinds of activities do you usually do ?
A: 无论多忙，我都抽时间来锻炼。
B: 哦，你一般都做什么运动?

A: How often do you go to the gym?
B: Once a week.
A: 你多久去一次健身房？
B: 一周一次。

🔵 情景单词快记忆

lose weight 减肥	overdo 把……做得过分
sore 痛的	muscle 肌肉
membership fee 会员费	fitness center 健身中心
enroll 加入	warm up 热身
exercise bike 骑车器	crowded 拥挤的
personal trainer 私人教练	squeeze 挤出
gym 健身房	sign up for 报名
membership 会员资格	quote 报价
locker room 更衣室	go to the gym 去健身房
pay a membership fee 交会员费用	activity 运动

读书笔记

27 社会议题
Social Issues

① 环保意识 Environment

高频单句大放送

01. I'm going green.
我要走向环保绿化。

02. I think I recycle more than I throw away.
我觉得我循环利用的东西比我扔掉的东西要多。

03. Are you trying to help the environment?
你在试着改善环境吗?

04. More and more people have realized environment problems.
越来越多的人已经意识到环境问题。

05. It's fantastic to be around so many people who care about the environment.
周围有那么多人都在关注环境,真是太好了。

06. I want to save more energy. I turn out the lights when I leave a room.
我想节省更多的能源。当我离开房间的时候会把灯关掉。

07. Wherever we go, we can find rubbish carelessly disposed.
无论我们走到哪里,都能看到随意丢弃的垃圾。

08. Are you doing anything to help the environment?
你做了什么事来帮助保护环境吗?

09. Massive destruction of environment has brought about negative effect.
环境的严重破坏已经带来了负面影响。

10. I'm going to ride my bike around more often, so I save money on gas and pollute less the air.
我经常骑自行车,所以我节省了汽油钱,也减少了污染。

口语问答面对面

A: I'm going green.
B: That's cool. Maybe I'll do the same.
A: 我要走向环保绿化。

B: 那很好，或许我也可以那么做。

A: Are you trying to help the environment?

B: Yeah, it's really important to me, so I've been doing a lot.

A: 你在试着改善环境吗?

B: 是啊，这对于我来说很重要，所以我做了很多。

A: More and more people have realized environment problems.

B: It's fantastic to be around so many people who care about the environment.

A: 越来越多的人已经意识到环境问题。

B: 周围有那么多人都在关注环境，真是太好了。

A: I want to save more energy. I turn out the lights when I leave a room.

B: Yeah, and it lowers your electric bill.

A: 我想节省更多的能源。当我离开房间的时候会把灯关掉。

B: 是的，这样可以减少电费。

A: Wherever we go, we can find rubbish carelessly disposed.

B: Maybe we could get involved in projects to improve the environment.

A: 无论我们走到哪里，都能看到随意丢弃的垃圾。

B: 或许我们可以参加一些项目来改善环境。

A: Factories always pollute the environment by pouring waste water directly into rivers.

B: I think we must take actions to solve environmental problems.

A: 工厂经常将废水直接排进河里，污染环境。

B: 我觉得我们必须采取行动解决环境问题。

A: Massive destruction of environment has brought about negative effect.

B: You're very right. Governments should focus on the preservation of the environment.

A: 环境的严重破坏已经带来了负面影响。

B: 你说得非常正确。政府应该注重环境保护。

A: Are you doing anything to help the environment?

B: I'm not too worried about it.

A: 你做了什么事来帮助保护环境吗?

B: 我不是很担心环境。

情景单词快记忆

environment 环境	organic food 有机食物
chemicals 化学物质	pesticide 杀虫剂
organic 有机的	bin 箱子
trash 垃圾	recycle 回收
litter 垃圾	conserve 节省
pollute 污染	protect 保护
tissues 纸巾	disposable 用完即丢弃的
dispose 处理	take action 采取行动
focus on 关注	preservation 保护
negative 消极的	bring about 引起
destruction 破坏	

② 博客 Blog

高频单句大放送

01. I like to follow celebrities' blogs.
我喜欢看名人的博客。

02. Are you a blogger?
你是博客写手吗？

03. When did you start blogging?
你什么时候开始写博客的？

04. How often do you publish a blog?
你多久发表一篇博客日志？

05. I need help with my blog layout. I don't know any HTML.
帮我设计个博客吧。我对 HTML 一点都不懂。

06. My friend has a really interesting blog.
我朋友有一个很有趣的博客。

07. I had an amazing weekend. I wrote all about it in my blog.
这个周末太有意思了。我把它全部写在博客里了。

08. I want to start up my own blog.
我想开通自己的博客。

09. Her blog received one million hits in less than four months.

她的博客在不到四个月点击量就达到了 100 万了。

10. I keep myself updated with my favorite stars by reading their blogs.
    我通过看我喜欢的名人的博客来了解他们的消息。

口语问答面对面

A: I want to start up my own blog.
B: Go for it. I'll be sure to read it.
A: 我想开通自己的博客。
B: 开通吧。我肯定会看的。

A: Her blog received one million hits in less than four months.
B: Cool. I might read it too. Send me the link.
A: 她的博客在不到四个月点击量就达到了 100 万了。
B: 好酷啊。我也应该看看，发给我链接吧。

A: My weekend was insane! I wrote an entry in my blog about it.
B: Cool, I'll have to read it.
A: 这个周末太疯狂了! 我在博客上记录下来了。
B: 太好了，我得去看看。

A: More and more movie stars are running their own blogs.
B: Yeah, and I keep myself updated with my favorite stars by reading their blogs.
A: 越来越多的影视明星开通了他们的博客。
B: 是啊，我通过看我喜欢的名人的博客来了解他们的消息。

A: Blogging is a good way to share your thoughts with others.
B: That's right. Blogging helps me feel more connected with others and increases my own sense of well-being and happiness.
A: 写博客是与他人分享思想的好方法。
B: 没错，写博客让我觉得与他人有更多的联系，让我感觉更幸福、更快乐。

A: My friend has a really interesting blog.
B: Can I have the link to it? I want to read it.
A: 我朋友有一个很有趣的博客。
B: 能把链接发给我吗? 我想看看。

A: Are you updating your blog?

B: Nah. I don't have time to write blogs.

A: 你仍在更新博客吗？

B: 没有。我没有时间写博客。

A: I am a newbie at blogging.

B: Well, I enjoy blogging, but I am a lurker.

A: 我是个博客新手。

B: 哦，我喜欢博客，但我只是个潜水者。

A: I want a web designer for my blog.

B: I have a few friends that could help you.

A: 我想请一个网页设计师来设计我的博客。

B: 我有几个朋友可以帮你。

A: I like to follow celebrities blogs.

B: I do the same thing.

A: 我喜欢看名人的博客。

B: 我也这么做。

🔵 情景单词快记忆

start up 开通	blog 博客
newbie 网络新手	lurker 潜水者
update 更新	nah 没有
blogging 写博客	insane 疯狂的
publish 发表	celebrity 名人
entry 记录	coding 编码
layout 设计	run one's blog 开通博客
read one's blog 读某人的博客	link 链接
hit 点击量	

③ 减肥 Losing Weight

🔵 高频单句大放送

01. I think I'm gaining weight.
    我觉得我长胖了。

02. Actually many people gain weight by drinking too much soda.
实际上很多人长胖是因为喝了太多汽水。

03. I am on a strict diet, so I can't eat too much.
我在厉行节食，所以我不能吃太多。

04. You might not believe this, but I used to be twice the size as I am now!
你可能不相信，但我以前确实比现在胖一倍。

05. I have tried to control my appetite, too, but I love eating very sweet stuff.
我也得尽量控制我的食欲，但我就是喜欢吃甜食。

06. I really want to lose some weight.
我真的想减肥。

07. I want to try and lose a few pounds.
我想争取减几磅。

08. You don't need to lose weight. You're fine how you are.
你不需要减肥。你现在的体重正好。

09. I'm back down to my ideal weight.
我又回到我的理想体重了。

10. The doctor said I have been eating too much.
医生说我吃得太多了。

口语问答面对面

A: I think I'm gaining weight.
B: You should not drink soda. Actually many people gain weight by drinking too much soda.
A: 我觉得我长胖了。
B: 你不应该喝汽水。实际上很多人长胖是因为喝了太多汽水。

A: You might not believe this, but I used to be twice the size as I am now!
B: Really? I hope jogging can keep my weight down then.
A: 你可能不相信，但我以前确实比现在胖一倍。
B: 真的吗? 那我希望慢跑可以让我的体重减下去。

A: I am on a strict diet, so I can't eat too much.
B: Well, I have tried to control my appetite, too, but I love eating very sweet stuff.
A: 我在厉行节食，所以我不能吃太多。
B: 我也得尽量控制我的食欲，但我就是喜欢吃甜食。

A: The doctor said I have been eating too much.
B: So you're going on a diet.
A: 医生说我吃得太多了。
B: 所以你在节食。

A: I want to try and lose a few pounds.
B: I'll help you out if you need it.
A: 我想争取减几磅。
B: 如果你需要，我会帮你的。

A: Do you think I'm gaining weight? I feel like I'm heavier than I used to be.
B: Well, maybe a little. But it's no big deal.
A: 你觉得我变胖了吗? 我感觉我比以前重了。
B: 可能有点。但没什么大不了的。

A: I'm supposed to be slimming.
B: I'll help you out if you need it.
A: 我需要减肥。
B: 如果你需要，我会帮你的。

A: I know I'm getting a little tummy.
B: It's not too bad.
A: 我知道我有点小肚子了。
B: 还不是太糟糕。

A: I'm back down to my ideal weight.
B: Congrats!Let's celebrate.
A: 我又回到我的理想体重了。
B: 恭喜你! 咱们庆祝一下吧。

🔵 情景单词快记忆

gain weight 增肥	lose weight 减肥
pound 磅	thinner 更瘦
balanced diet 均衡饮食	effective 有效的
go on a diet 节食	thanks to 由于
congratulation 恭喜	obese 极为肥胖的

soda 汽水	slimming 苗条的
tummy 肚子	appetite 食欲
jog 慢跑	health food 保健食品
racket 骗局	sweet stuff 甜食
control 控制	lose some weight 减肥

读书笔记

28 体育盛事
Sports Event

① 伦敦奥运会 London Olympic Games

🔵 高频单句大放送

01. What are the aims of the Olympics?
奥运会的目的是什么？

02. What is the most distinct symbol of the Olympic Games?
奥运会最显著的标志是什么？

03. What's the origin of the Olympics?
奥运会的起源是什么？

04. The Olympic Flame represents the continuity between the ancient and modern Games.
奥林匹克圣火代表着古代奥运会和现代奥运会之间的延续。

05. The Olympic games originated from ancient Greece. They were a part of a religious festival in honour of the God Zeus.
奥运会源于古希腊。它是纪念宙斯之神的宗教节日的一部分。

06. What's the Olympic Flame?
奥林匹克圣火是什么？

07. Where will these Olympic Games be held?
这届的奥运会将在哪里举行？

08. We hope that the Olympic Games will be increasingly pure, and return to the spirit of "Faster, Higher and Stronger"!
希望奥运精神越来越简单纯洁，回归到奥林匹克"更快、更高、更强"的精神上来！

09. I am going to London for the Olympic Game.
我要去伦敦参加奥运会。

10. Which city held the summer Olympic Games in 1908?
1908 年的夏季奥运会是在哪个城市举办的？

口语问答面对面

A: What is the most distinct symbol of the Olympic Games?

B: That is a piece of cake. The five rings.

A: 奥运会最显著的标志是什么?

B: 太容易了，五环呀。

A: What are the aims of the Olympics?

B: The aims are firstly to develop and promote peace, understanding and friendship between countries; secondly to bring together the best athletes in the world every four years.

A: 奥运会的目的是什么?

B: 奥运会的目的，第一是发展和推动国与国之间的和平、理解和友谊，第二是为了每四年使全世界最优秀的运动员欢聚一堂。

A: What's the origin of the Olympics?

B: The Olympic games originated from ancient Greece. They were a part of a religious festival in honour of the God Zeus.

A: 奥运会的起源是什么?

B: 奥运会源于古希腊。它是纪念宙斯之神的宗教节日的一部分。

A: What's the Olympic Flame?

B: The Olympic Flame represents the continuity between the ancient and modern Games.

A: 奥林匹克圣火是什么?

B: 奥林匹克圣火代表着古代奥运会和现代奥运会之间的延续。

A: Where can I get the time-table for shuttle buses?

B: You can get it from the Information Center.

A: 在哪里可以领到班车时刻表?

B: 在信息中心。

A: Where will these Olympic Games be held?

B: In London.

A: 这届的奥运会将在哪里举行?

B: 伦敦。

A: Where are you going?

B: I am going to London for the Olympic Games.

A: 你要去哪?
B: 我要去伦敦参加奥运会。

A: Long time no see! Where have you been?
B: I went to London for the competition.
A: 好久没见了! 你去哪儿了?
B: 我去伦敦参加奥运会了。

A: Which city held the summer Olympic Games in 1908?
B: London, in England.
A: 1908 年的夏季奥运会是在哪个城市举办的?
B: 英国伦敦。

🔵 情景单词快记忆

game 比赛	distinct 显著的
symbol 象征	represent 代表
flag 旗帜	sign 标志
slogan 口号	design 构思
participate 参加	champion 冠军
committee 委员会	athlete 运动员
medal 奖章	origin 起源
promote 推动	emblem 徽章
motto 箴言	arrangement 布置
beat 打败	indicate 标示

② 田径赛 Track and Field

🔵 高频单句大放送

01. Could you tell me what's the difference between track and field?
你能告诉我竞赛与田赛的区别吗?

02. What event are you in?
你是从事什么项目的?

03. I'm very disappointed at not getting a chance to compete in the final.
我很失望，我没机会进入决赛了。

04. It's a bad beginning. But I hope that I can perform well in the next event.
不好的开头。但我希望接下来的比赛中能表现好。

05. The world women's 5,000 meters record is broken.
女子5000米世界纪录被打破了。

06. Who broke it?
谁打破的?

07. He is a discus thrower.
他是掷铁饼的。

08. Will Liu Xiang participate in the London Olympics?
刘翔会参加伦敦奥运会吗?

09. It is said that Liu Xiang will retire after the London Olympics.
据说刘翔在伦敦奥运会之后将要退役。

10. Is he a high jumper?
他是跳高的吗?

口语问答面对面

A: What event are you in?
B: Decathlon.
A: 你是从事什么项目的?
B: 田径十项全能运动。

A: Could you tell me what's the difference between track and filed?
B: Athletic events are divided into two broad categories—track and field. Each has its particular events.
A: 你能告诉我竞赛与田赛的区别吗?
B: 运动项目分为两个大类——竞赛与田赛。每一个都有其特定的项目。

A: What's wrong? You look pale.
B: I failed in the preliminary for the 100-meterdash. I was rather disappointed at my performance yesterday.
A: 怎么了? 你看上去脸色苍白。
B: 我在百米预赛中失利了。我对昨天的表现很失望。

A: I'm sorry to hear that.
B: I'm very disappointed at not getting a chance to compete in the final.
A: 很遗憾听到这个消息。
B: 我很失望, 我没机会进入决赛了。

A: What a pity. But you still have your 200-meter race.

B: It's a bad beginning. But I hope that I can perform well in the next event.

A: 真遗憾！但你还有 200 米比赛。

B: 不好的开头。但我希望接下来的比赛中能表现好。

A: Is there anything new today?

B: Yes. The world women's 5,000 meters record is broken.

A: 今天有什么新鲜事儿吗？

B: 有。女子 5000 米世界纪录被打破了。

A: Who broke it?

B: I don't know her name. But she is a new one and runs much faster.

A: 谁打破的？

B: 我不知道她的名字。但她是个新手，跑得相当快。

A: Is he a high jumper?

B: No. He is a discus thrower.

A: 他是跳高的吗？

B: 不，他是掷铁饼的。

A: Do you know Liu Xiang?

B: Of course. He is our Chinese's pride.

A: 你知道刘翔吗？

B: 当然了。他是我们中国人的骄傲。

A: Will Liu Xiang participate in the London Olympics?

B: He certainly will.

A: 刘翔会参加伦敦奥运会吗？

B: 当然了。

A: It is said that LiuXiang will retire after the London Olympic.

B: I'm sorry to hear that.

A: 据说刘翔在伦敦奥运会之后将要退役。

B: 太可惜了。

🔵 情景单词快记忆

broadcast 广播	terrific 极好的

jump 跳	extra 额外的
height 高度	hurdle 栏架
marathon 马拉松	cheer 欢呼
optimum 最适宜的	accelerate 加速
sprint 短跑	preliminary 预赛
posture 姿势	stamina 持久力
feat 业绩	capture 夺得
perfect 完美的	tournament 锦标赛
inaugurate 开始；进行	

③ 体操 Gymnastic

🔵 高频单句大放送

01. Oh, hollow flyaway.
噢，直体后空翻下。

02. What is the optimum starting age for a young gymnast?
少年儿童从事体操运动的最佳起始年龄为多大？

03. How many countries have participated in this tournament?
有多少国家参加了本届比赛？

04. In recent years female gymnasts have reached their peak between the age of fourteen and sixteen.
最近几年女子体操运动员达到顶峰时期的年龄在 14 到 16 岁。

05. How well she times every movement with the music.
她的动作与音乐节奏配合得多好啊！

06. When was the tournament inaugurated?
该项比赛是什么时候开始的？

07. Are there any top gymnasts competing in this year's China Cup?
本届中国杯赛有没有顶级运动员参加？

08. There comes my favorite gymnast.
我最喜欢的运动员上场了。

09. What are the physical qualities that a good gymnast requires?
优秀体操运动员对身体素质的要求是什么？

10. A good gymnast requires strength, stamina, flexibility, coordination, spring, speed, balance, a sense of rhythm and good posture.

优秀体操运动员需要有力量、耐力、柔韧、协调、弹跳力、速度、平衡、节奏感和良好的姿态。

口语问答面对面

A: Oh, hollow flyaway.

B: You see, his landing is both swift and sure.

A: 噢，直体后空翻下。

B: 你看，他落地又快又稳。

A: She's balancing herself on the strength of a single arm.

B: It takes a lot of skill and physical strength to do that, doesn't it?

A: 她仅用一只手臂的力量保持着整个身体的平衡。

B: 这需要有高超的技术和体力，对吧？

A: What is the optimum starting age for a young gymnast?

B: The optimum starting age is eight.

A: 少年儿童从事体操运动的最佳起始年龄为多大？

B: 最佳起始年龄是 8 岁。

A: When does a young gymnast reach her peak?

B: In recent years female gymnasts have reached their peak between the age of fourteen and sixteen.

A: 女子少年运动员多大可以达到最高水平？

B: 最近几年女子体操运动员达到顶峰时期的年龄在 14 到 16 岁。

A: Has he ever won the world champion?

B: Yes. Several times. And last year he won the world championship of IAAC.

A: 他得过世界冠军吗？

B: 得过。都得过好几次了。他去年获得的是个人全能冠军。

A: How well she times every movement with the music.

B: Now she's off the beam.

A: 她的动作与音乐节奏配合得多好啊！

B: 现在，她要下来了。

A: When was the tournament inaugurated?

B: It began in 1988.

A: 该项比赛是什么时候开始的？

B: 是从 1988 年开始举办的。

A: Are there any top gymnasts competing in this year's China Cup?
B: Yes.
A: 本届中国杯赛有没有优秀运动员参加?
B: 有的。

A: There comes my favorite gymnast.
B: Quite smart. How old is he? Can you guess?
A: 我最喜欢的运动员上场了。
B: 挺帅的嘛，你猜他多大年纪?

情景单词快记忆

reach one's peak 达到最高水平	participate in 参加
Beijing Capital Gymnasium 北京首都体育馆	China Cup International Gymnastics Tournament 中国杯国际体操锦标赛
gymnastics 体操	piked jump 屈体跳
buck 弓背跃起	running on toes 足尖跑
high bar 高杠	shoulder stand 肩倒立
hanging bar 吊杠	sonersault 侧空翻
hand ring 吊环	required routine 规定动作
bar 横杠	bounding table 蹦床
parallel bars 双杠	pommel horse 鞍马
uneven bars 高低杠	balance beam 平衡木

读书笔记